HOOSIERS and Scrubby Dutch:
★ St. Louis's South Side ★

★ By Jim Merkel ★

REEDY PRESS
St. Louis, Missouri

Reedy Press
PO Box 5131
St. Louis, MO 63139, USA

Library of Congress Control Number: 2010933073
ISBN: 978-1-933370-62-0

Please visit our website at www.reedypress.com.

Design by Jill Halpin

Printed in the United States of America
10 11 12 13 14   5 4 3 2 1

Photo Credits:
(Unless noted below, all photos are from the author or publisher)
Arteaga Photos: 29
Carondelet Historical Society: 1, 8-9 (Ironclads), 18-20, 54, 111
Slim Cox: 27
Dogtown Historical Society archives: 137
Library of Congress: 8-9 (Eads), 15, 56, 67, 116
Mickey McTague: 30-31
Bruce Marren: 22-23
National Weather Service: 121
Don Roussin: 115, 124, 125
Jim Shrewsbury: 45
Sinclair Ford: 32
Steve Mizerany: 34-35
Strosnider family: 59
Tower Grove Park: 88-89

Contents

PLACES   57

EVENTS   117

UNUSUAL, UNIQUE,
OR JUST PLAIN ODD   143

Preface

Call me a stubborn German. Find me someplace I like, and I'll settle in and won't leave. Maybe that's why we've lived in a house in the Bevo Mill neighborhood for eighteen years. We've fixed it the way we like and have no plans to leave. The office where I worked for the *Suburban Journals* for fifteen years is five minutes away on Chippewa Street. All that time, I worked in the same cubicle. Around me, the world went crazy, but peace reigned in that corner of the universe. I would still be there if the *Journals* didn't close the office, dismantle the cubicle, and send me to a new office in far West County in 2009. Change isn't in me. It's no coincidence the house and the office were on the South Side. For a century and a half, five generations of Merkels have spent part of their lives in St. Louis south of where Highway 40 is today.

My great-great grandfather brought his family to St. Louis in 1858 and started a piano factory around Park Avenue and South Broadway. He was one of thousands of German immigrants who came to the city in the middle of the 1800s. He eventually moved the business to an exclusive district near the Old Courthouse but died in 1885 at his home south of downtown. His son followed him into the business and lived east of Lafayette Square with his wife, my grandfather, and three other children. They lived east of where a monster tornado rammed through the city in 1896, killing 255 people. The stories they must have told. My great aunt had a beauty shop on Cherokee Street.

After my mother died, my dad remarried and moved with his second wife into her brick gingerbread-style house on Haven Street west of Carondelet Park. My brother lives near McCausland and Manchester avenues. There's plenty of the South Side on my mother's side, too. Her mother grew up in a house on Idaho Avenue. Today, it's within sight of Interstate 55 and the Loughborough Commons Shopping Center. After he married my grandmother, my mother's father had a hardware store at Arsenal Street and Grand Boulevard in the 1920s.

No wonder I heard so much about the South Side as I grew up. I heard about the Scrubby Dutch, shopped at Hampton Village, ate at Rigazzi's, and learned to keep away from no-account hoosiers. I learned how preservationists saved the Chatillon-DeMenil Mansion from demolition meant to make way for Interstate 55. When a museum opened there in 1965, my father—another piano man—donated a piano my great-great grandfather made at Park and Broadway. My brother—the fifth generation in the business—has since worked on restoring that square piano. It's still there.

We strayed to the county and beyond but always returned. I ventured to Pennsylvania before I brought my wife back in 1991. A year later, we moved to the Bevo Mill neighborhood. By then, I worked for the *Suburban Journals*. I transferred to the office near my house in 1994 and started covering the South Side in 2001. I love community journalism, but what could be better than practicing it in a place like South St. Louis? Since then, my interviews with hundreds of St. Louisans living south of Highway 40 gave me a true appreciation of the place and of the people.

Now Reedy Press has given me even more of a chance to find out about South Siders by allowing me to write a book about this place. I'm thrilled. I tasted a brain sandwich at Ferguson's Pub. I'm glad I did it but won't do it again, thanks. I spent a Saturday afternoon with Mickey McTague at Shaw Coffee. I heard women at the Altenheim who were approaching the century mark talking about the days when women scrubbed concrete steps. One remembered my grandfather's hardware store. I spent hours at the St. Louis Public Library's Central Library downtown going through microfilm of old newspapers. All of this confirmed what I have long thought: South Siders are down-to-earth, good people. No, they're not perfect, but they've made the South Side a place like nowhere else. I'm staying until they drag me away for good. But, as I said, I'm a stubborn German.

Introduction

With a mix of Cardinals and Anheuser-Busch memorabilia draping the walls, Ferguson's Pub at 2925 Mount Pleasant Street is as South Side as it gets. Throw in the fact that it is one of the last places to buy a genuine brain sandwich, and the restaurant should be a great inspiration when it comes to defining the South Side of St. Louis, as well as South Siders.

A patron sat at the bar and tried to explain. "If you don't know what makes it the South Side, you're not a South Sider," he said. "If you weren't born and raised on the South Side, I can't explain it to you." The man's explanation may seem to be influenced by drink, but what he said makes sense. It's hard to explain what makes the South Side the South Side.

To be sure, South St. Louis City occupies a special place in the Metropolitan St. Louis area. Whether they have relocated to Arnold, St. Charles, or Collinsville, people reared on the South Side always bring with them fond remembrances of life south of Highway 40. Most remember living in an old house in a lot so small they could look out a side window into their neighbor's window. They remember Ted Drewes, Carondelet Park, and Southtown Famous. If they're older, Cherokee Street and Casa Loma may come to mind. The city's mayor, himself a child of the South Side, has his own memories. "We had all kinds of personalities, people from different religious backgrounds," Francis G. Slay said in his office at City Hall. He hesitated to characterize the South Sider. "Virtually any type of character you had on the South Side." Slay recalls the neighborhoods as tight, where everyone knew everybody. "It was, I think, a very good place to grow up and raise a family."

More than that, it was a place to feast on different neighborhoods close to each other. Carondelet is nothing like Shaw. The ranch homes of St. Louis Hills Estates are nothing like the two-story brick homes of Dutchtown. The mansions in Compton Heights look nothing like the frame houses in Bevo Mill. The international shopping district on South Grand Boulevard is much different from busy Hampton Avenue. It's said that if you don't like the weather in St. Louis, wait five minutes, and it'll change.

If you're driving on the South Side, you don't need five minutes. Wait a minute, and you'll see something new. There are few places in the metropolitan area with so many different kinds of neighborhoods set so close together.

History not only played a role in making these places so different, but it also brought factors that many held in common. One of the biggest was the Catholic faith. Another was race: the South Side still is heavily white. "You're talking about a white working class community," said Mark Abbott, a professor of history with urban emphasis at Harris-Stowe State University. He is a resident of the Tower Grove South neighborhood and the author of the book *Tower Grove*, about neighborhoods around Tower Grove Park. Abbott sees similarities between the South Side and parts of some other cities. Places in East Coast cities like South Philadelphia, South Boston, and Queens are among them, he said. "South Boston is very Irish. South Philly is pretty Italian," he said. South Milwaukee is another similar community, he said. Such places give rise to characters in politics, in churches, across the street. And characters lead to stories, some of which are repeated here.

In recent years, many of the stories had to do with how much of the South Side has turned itself around. Ten, twenty, thirty, and forty years ago, much of the South Side was in severe distress. But, as many of the stories in this volume testify, one by one the neighborhoods, parks, and commercial districts breathed new life. Tax breaks and the work of the mayor and aldermen helped, but what really made it happen were individuals who saw the potential of their area and worked to improve it. One of the first was Lafayette Square. It went from an area full of tenements and prostitutes to a revitalized stately Victorian neighborhood set around a park. Ruth Kamphoefner's story recounted in these pages is representative of the many individuals who bought broken-down Victorian homes for next to nothing and devoted much of their lives rehabbing them. The rehabbers went from home to home saving them from demolition.

Tower Grove Park came back under Director John Karel. Immigrants and refugees with a vision turned the South Grand commercial district into a vibrant international shopping and restaurant mecca. Bosnian refugees who came in the 1990s are doing the same in the area around the Bevo Mill. Hispanics settled in the former shopping area of Cherokee Street west of Jefferson Avenue and made it their own. Those who see history in one hundred-year-old tables and chairs turned Cherokee Street east of Jefferson into the best place in the region to look for antiques.

Young professionals did their part by purchasing, maintaining, and improving homes on the South Side, many of which were saved by rehabbers, who do their work on just about every street south of Highway 40. The work slowed considerably when the recession started. Condos went unsold, and previously announced projects never got started. But even in the worst of the recession, individuals assured that the South Side would keep improving. Everywhere the story is the same. The South Side still has a way to go, but those with negative impressions made decades ago may be surprised at what they discover when they drive around South St. Louis with open eyes for an afternoon.

The impetus of the rehabbers was the availability of abandoned or low-cost housing, mixed with high-quality brick construction. The low prices and abandonment were the result of a lowered population. For fifty years, people moved out. Then after 2000, we're told, the city actually gained a few people. We won't really know if this is true until the results of the 2010 census are released, but it seems the days of emptying out have largely passed on the South Side. The suburbs are fine, if you like that, but those who remain prefer the urban life to the suburban. They like their homes close together and stop signs that really don't stop anybody. They like being minutes from Ted Drewes or the Hill. To them, life on the South Side is like going around all the time in their favorite pair of old shoes. As the guy in the bar said, that still may not explain what it means to be a South Sider. Maybe he's right. Maybe if you don't know what makes it the South Side, you're not a South Sider. Maybe if you weren't born and raised on the South Side, then nobody can explain it. For those who don't understand, the stories in this book may help. Those who do will find that the stories affirm their convictions. Read on.

*Bob Burnes addresses
an audience at a CSMAC
groundbreaking.*

⭐ PEOPLE ⭐

Hoosiers

On a warm Saturday in April 2010, about two-dozen people on the South Side of St. Louis paused to ponder a question many have considered before them. Just what exactly is a hoosier? "It's one of those things. It's like pornography. You know it when you see it," St. Louis Hills resident Courtney Wheaton said at a family picnic in Willmore Park. Holly Hills resident Mike Carril put down his vanilla shake at Ted Drewes to form an answer. They're "somebody that doesn't secure their property. They've just got bad habits. They're loud and rowdy." To Julie McNeal, a news editor for KSDK-Channel 5, a hoosier is white trash. A hoosier would have his hair with short sides and top and long hair on the back and wear tight, tight jeans and high-topped tennis shoes, she said outside the Soulard Farmer's Market. "They'd be very right-wing. Beer, guns, and ammo," the forty-year-old Benton Park resident said.

Nearby, Norma King, seventy-three, of the Compton Hill Reservoir Square neighborhood, offered that the term was derogatory. "I really don't like to pigeonhole people," she said. At the Time Out Bar and Grill, 3805 Meramec Street, a man named Glenn stopped watching a game between the Cardinals and the Mets to say the word means "trash." But then the Dutchtown-area man added that the word was unfair. "To be called a hoosier is an insulting term." Back in Willmore Park, a man took umbrage at the question. "You callin' me a (expletive) hoosier?"

The meaning is enough to start a fight in some places around here, but nowhere else. When people outside of the St. Louis region think of the word, they conjure up the positive image of the Indiana hoosier, but that wasn't always so. Jeffrey Graf took time off from his job with the reference department of the Herman B. Wells Library of Indiana University–Bloomington to study how the word came to be, with all of its good and bad overtones. "The best evidence, however, suggests that 'hoosier' was a term of contempt and opprobrium common in the upland South and used to denote a rustic, a bumpkin, a countryman, a roughneck, a hick or an awkward, uncouth or unskilled fellow," he wrote. In other words, a South Side hoosier.

Graf offered various reasons for the way the word began. One is that when the state of Indiana was being laid out, surveyors who found the residence of a squatter would ask, "Who's here?" Others believe it is a derogatory word used in the South for an uncouth rustic. One possibility is that *hoosier* often was used throughout the South in the nineteenth century to mean woodsmen or rough hill people. A similar word *hoozer* is used in the dialect of Cumberland, England, for hill dwellers or highlands. They settled in the Cumberland Mountains, Cumberland River, and Cumberland Gap and in the hills of southern Indiana.

As for the St. Louis exception to the generally good view of hoosiers, Graf points to a study by Kansas State University English professor Thomas E. Murray. "Few epithets in St. Louis carry the pejorative connotations or the potential for eliciting negative responses that hoosier does," Murray wrote. Some in St. Louis and on the South Side may see a hoosier as someone who has shown a bad side. Others may say that's unfair. A third group of South Siders holds on to the title "South Side Hoosier." They don't mean it in the Indiana sense. They keep up their property as well as anyone but laugh at the idea of being associated with the uncouth. Mickey McTague, a lifetime South Sider who's worked with politicians, entertainers, and others, sees the title as a way to connect with victims of bigotry. "South St. Louis has been unfairly defamed in many ways," he said. "I'm very proud to say that I'm a South Side hoosier."

Unquestionably, the word is derogatory, but in a time when most people have stopped using almost all derogatory names for racial, religious, or ethnic groups, this one remains in use on the South Side and in the rest of the area. It may be that the term doesn't refer to who people are but what the Reverend Martin Luther King Jr. called "the content of their character." Whatever it is, the description by blues musician Van Johnson of a hoosier is typical. "A hoosier is when they throw their trash out the window," the Carondelet neighborhood resident said, taking a break from playing for tips near the Soulard Farmer's Market. "They don't cut their lawn. Basically, just people that like to barbecue every day, get fat, and do nothing."

Scrubby Dutch

A hapless Fuller Brush salesman once asked Florence Deppe if she wanted to buy a mop. Absolutely not, she replied. She gets down on her knees with a brush and does her cleaning that way, she told him. "He said, 'I hear the same story all along here,'" Deppe relayed. "Nobody in South St. Louis uses a mop," he said with a sigh. Deppe was just months from being one hundred years old when she told the story about the ways of the South Side Scrubby Dutch. She related it in the dining room of the St. Louis Altenheim, a senior citizens assisted-living facility at 5408 South Broadway. It was lunchtime, and Deppe and other Altenheim residents were eating salad, melons, spaghetti, and cake near a floor-to-ceiling window that reveals one of the best views of the Mississippi south of the Arch. All remembered growing up and living in South St. Louis in the early to middle part of the twentieth century, when people regularly cleaned steps and sometimes sidewalks with soapy brushes.

"Every Saturday, they'd get out there and scrub the sidewalks," said Betty Reinbold, who is eighty-nine. Those who lived in flats with more than one tenant took turns. "If you didn't do it, you weren't worth anything," said Reinbold, who lived in a house on Minnesota Avenue that was later demolished by the builders of Interstate 55. She doesn't remember sidewalks being scrubbed as much as she remembers steps being scrubbed. "I don't think it mattered what they were. They got scrubbed." When she first married, she and her husband lived in a flat on Chippewa Street. They took turns cleaning the concrete steps. But she eased up when she and her husband bought a home on Austria Street. "I didn't scrub them. I washed them off with a hose."

Deppe recalled a man would come by every Saturday to scrub her family's concrete front porch with Bon Ami. "I think my mother gave him a dollar," she said. "Of course everybody on the block hired him and so the whole block had a fresh appearance." Virginia Palazzolo, who is ninety-eight and grew up on Hartford Street one block east of Grand, has memories of cleaning her family's porch, which was wooden on the top and concrete on the bottom. "We'd get on our hands and knees and scrub it with a brush," said Palazzolo. She believes the preferred soap was Fels Naptha. Her recollection also is that she used a hose and a broom for the concrete steps. "It was just in their heritage, I guess, to keep everything neat and clean."

Esley Hamilton, a historian working for St. Louis County, believes the Scrubby Dutch practice may hearken back to a time when people dragged a lot more dirt into the house. Hamilton, who specializes in the preservation of historic buildings, said the front limestone steps would have shown dirt more. "The streets were dirty. There were no paved streets," Hamilton said. Since there were no vacuum cleaners to suck up dirt, housewives wanted to scrub as much of it off the steps as they could before it had a chance to come in.

That may or may not have led people living around Marion Bolt's house to get on their knees and scrub slab concrete steps. Bolt, who is ninety-two, lives in the Maryville Apartments at 4257 Nebraska Avenue. After she married in 1937, she and her husband moved to a house at 4727 Parker Avenue. "They did it as far back as I can remember," Bolt said. "Every Friday they would be out scrubbing the steps." And what did they scrub the steps with? Dutch Cleanser, of course.

The Horse Thieves of Carondelet

The town of Carondelet developed just to the south of St. Louis, but at a much slower pace. Some Carondelet families take pride in the fact that they can trace their lineage back to the independent nineteenth-century township. For the most part, the history of the town and these families is rich and vibrant, but there was a devious side. The evidence comes from "Carondelet Yesterday and Today," an unpublished manuscript written in 1933 that is on the shelves of the St. Louis Public Library's Central Branch. The author, A. Ryrie Koch, writes that robbery and horse thievery were problems in Carondelet as early as 1840. One Frenchman named Louis was especially frightening to horse owners. "If a man was riding one that this desperado fancied, it was worth the rider's life if he did not give it up," Koch wrote. He was gone by 1846, when the citizenry could rest.

Koch also told of a company of horse thieves, led by a man named Sanspeur, who brought the citizenry endless grief. Whenever someone's horse was missing, Sanspeur would appear and offer to find it, for a small fee of five dollars. The man who paid the money would be led to another person who would offer to help find it for another fee of five dollars. "After this had been repeated several times, the horse would be returned but usually in such a poor condition that the animal would not be worth the many five dollars paid," Koch wrote. When they were done stealing horses, the rogues had children who had children whose descendants today have yet to discover their ancestors' occupations.

A Failed Vision

In the 1840s, Charles Dickens was adding to his fame by writing about the cruelty of industrialization. Reformers reacted to that cruelty in different ways. Karl Marx thought economic communism would cure the excesses. Others retreated from society and formed communities they thought would be free of the evil they witnessed. Etienne Cabet, a politician, lawyer, and writer, published a novel around 1839 called *Voyage en Icarie*. In it, he laid out his utopian vision for a perfect life. This brought him thousands of followers, and some decided to go to America to follow their dreams in Icarian communities. One Icarian community settled on the south side of the present-day intersection of Hampton Avenue and Interstate 44.

In 1848, a group of Cabet's followers arrived in the Red River valley of Texas to bring the Icarian idea to the New World. Unfortunately, that land was too unhealthy to live in, but soon Cabet came to join them. Together, they came to the abandoned former Mormon settlement of Navoo, Illinois, to establish their community. A branch settlement was established in Adams County, Iowa. However, many members saw Cabet's leadership style as dictatorial. In 1856, a majority of the Navoo community expelled Cabet. He brought about 180 of his followers to St. Louis. Shortly after the move, he died suddenly on November 8, 1856.

The community could have scattered, but it didn't. Members stayed to build the kind of community Cabet envisioned. They worked in St. Louis to provide for the community. In the spring of 1858, they bought property called Cheltenham six miles west of St. Louis, around the present location of Wilson Avenue east of Sulphur Avenue. They put $8,000 down on the $25,000 cost of the land and made regular monthly payments. The group had a band and a school, and they often put on plays promoting their ideals. They published a newspaper distributed around the world. But Icaria wouldn't last. Members started squabbling and leaving. The community fell behind on its mortgage. The end of the vision came in March of 1864 when the holder of the mortgage on their property demanded the group to either pay or give the land back. The Icarians couldn't pay, so they left the land. The utopians from Icaria scattered and had to make their way in a most capitalist of lands.

Secret Weapons in Carondelet

People here know James B. Eads as the man who did something the experts said couldn't be done: build a bridge across the Mississippi at St. Louis. Down south, he is known for ridding the Mississippi south of New Orleans of sandbars that clogged the river. That enabled New Orleans to become a major port. A third accomplishment is often overlooked. On the river in Carondelet, he made weapons that were key to the Union's control over the Mississippi River during the Civil War. Ironclads made at shipyards in Carondelet that fought their way past Confederate positions on the Mississippi, Ohio, and lesser rivers were impervious to the iron balls that cannons heaved at them.

Before the war, this self-taught engineer made his fortune salvaging sunken steamboats from the bottom of the river. He had retired and was looking forward to a life of leisure. But soon after Confederates fired on Fort Sumter in April 1861, Eads started arguing that a fleet of armored gunboats could help open the Mississippi River. Five days later, he received a telegram from a friend from St. Louis, U.S. Attorney General Edward Bates: "Be not surprised if you are called here suddenly by telegram." Eads's ideas won over Lincoln's cabinet. On August 7, 1861, Eads signed a contract to build seven gunboats ready for crews and arms within sixty-five days.

To build his boats, Eads leased some existing yards from Marceau Street to Catalan Street in the city of Carondelet. Called the Carondelet Marine Railways, it was established in 1857 as a place for building and repairing riverboats. He established another yard at Mound City, Illinois, on the Ohio River near Cairo. At those yards, he set about to build seven ironclad gunboats named for communities on the upper Mississippi and Ohio rivers. Boats made at Carondelet were key to the Union victory at the Confederate Fort Henry on the Tennessee River on February 6, 1862. It was more than a month before the Confederate ironclad the *Merrimack* and the Union ironclad the *Monitor* fought to a famous draw on March 8–9, 1862, at Hampton Roads, Virginia. Eads's boats went on to help win victories at Fort Donelson on the Cumberland River and elsewhere.

Anywhere from several hundred to four thousand people toiled at the Carondelet Works. Ron Bolte, who heads the Carondelet Historical Society, speculates the number was closer to two thousand. The works kept turning out iron boats that pushed south as Admiral David G. Farragut made his way northward from New Orleans. When a siege was broken at Vicksburg in July 1863, all of the river was in Union hands, but boats still were needed to go up smaller waterways in Arkansas. In 1863, Eads bought land on the river in Carondelet from Davis Avenue to Poepping Street. Carondelet promised Eads wouldn't have to pay property taxes if he stayed for five years. Bolte compares it to today's tax increment financing, in which tax money meant for schools or police instead is used for bonds for a shopping center or other project receiving special government sanctions.

Eventually, Eads produced about two-dozen boats that helped shorten the war. After he stopped producing boats when the war ended in 1865, Carondelet sued Eads for failing to live up to his part of the deal on the tax break. The city lost. In 1870, St. Louis swallowed the community. Meanwhile, the ironclads were used for scrap. One survived—the *Cairo*—but only because it sank after it hit a Confederate mine on December 12, 1862, north of Vicksburg. By being on the bottom of the river, it avoided those hungry for scrap. After the *Cairo* was found in 1956 under river silt, it was brought to the surface and placed on display at the Vicksburg Military Park in 1977. But it is not necessary to travel to Vicksburg to learn the significance of what the ironclads did on the Mississippi. The Carondelet Historical Society has a thorough exhibit on Eads's boats at its headquarters at 6303 Michigan Avenue. A plaque at South St. Louis Square Park at South Broadway and Courtois Street also speaks of his accomplishment in opening the Mississippi during the Civil War. South Siders can say with pride that Carondelet was the place where he performed this act to shorten the war.

A Confederate Attack or
a Flight of Fancy

It wasn't exactly the Battle of Gettysburg, and it wasn't even a Civil War
skirmish, but if the raid at the home of Cheltenham Postmaster Augustus
Muegge really happened, it would have meant Confederate guerillas
penetrated the future borders of St. Louis just months before the Civil
War was over. A newspaper that repeated the official report of the incident
also suggested that other factors may have clouded Muegge's memory.
Muegge claimed the raid happened between 5 and 6 p.m. on Wednesday,
September 28, 1864, at his home, general store, and post office on
Manchester Road. Had it not been torn down in 1905, that home today
would be at 6429 Manchester Avenue, on the corner of Dale Avenue and
Manchester. The Muegges had built their store and home in 1854 in an
area surrounded by slave-holding Southern planters. As the postmaster,
Muegge was seen as a Lincoln man.

This may have made him think the worst was coming when, he said,
four men wearing regular Confederate uniforms rode to his door. As the
Missouri Republican reported in its October 1, 1864, edition, two of those
men got off their horses and went into the store while two others stayed
outside with the horses. The two asked Muegge which side he was on. "I
am a Union man," the *Missouri Republican* reported Muegge as saying.
Then they asked him if he had held office in Lincoln's government.
"Yes—I hold office now. I am Postmaster here," Muegge answered. "It's
just such men as you that we want to kill," one of the two supposedly said.

Then one of them pulled out a revolver, cocked it, and pointed it at
Muegge. Before he could shoot, Muegge's wife got between them and
said that he'd have to kill her first. When the man tried to point over her
shoulder, she pushed the firearm away. Muegge ran out the door, found
a horse, and rode it to a military camp on Olive Street Road. There
he told his tale and said a similar group had been at a home two miles

away. Apparently, some didn't believe him. "Owing to the great delay on account of the incredibility of the story, the statement was not reported at headquarters until Friday morning," the *Missouri Republican* said. Then a scout was sent out. The *Missouri Republican* speculated that the Confederates were part of a group harassing the Pacific Railroad running west along Manchester, but it also noted that it was hard for Confederates to cross the fords and bridges along the Meramec River, since they all were well guarded. "The most plausible explanation is that the fright of the Postmaster induced him to imagine a great deal more than he saw and in his statement drew largely on his fancy," the paper said. If nothing else, it made for a good story of how a postmaster far from the fighting got involved in the battle to preserve the Union.

A Lawsuit for Henry Shaw

Henry Shaw never married, but the man who founded the Missouri Botanical Garden did have woman problems. One woman in particular sued him for a fortune for what she claimed was fudging on a promise to marry her. If she had won, the garden might not have looked as grand in its early years. The story shows the dangers of renting a piano to just any lady.

The tale is told in *Henry Shaw: His Life and Legacies* by renowned Saint Louis University Historian Father William Barnaby Faherty, S.J. In 1856, Shaw, a wealthy retired St. Louis hardware baron, prepared to open a botanical garden at his country home outside St. Louis. In February of that year, a woman named Effie Carstang borrowed one hundred dollars from Shaw. He had met her the year before and seemed fascinated by her loveliness. The next year, she borrowed an additional one hundred dollars from him. Then in August of 1857, she rented a piano from Shaw for one dollar a month.

It seemed harmless enough. But on July 19, 1858, she filed a suit in the St. Louis Court of Common Pleas for breach of promise of marriage. She asked for twenty thousand dollars in damages but then raised her demand to one hundred thousand dollars. She claimed they had promised to marry in 1856 after a friendship grew into romance. Shaw denied he had made any such promise. Effie and her sister contended the piano was a gift. If it was, Shaw took it back.

The two sides met in court on May 27, 1859, less than a month before the Missouri Botanical Garden opened. Effie was represented by criminal lawyer and state legislator Major Uriel L. Wright. Shaw's legal team included Edward Bates, who later became attorney general under President Abraham Lincoln. The jury heard testimony that Shaw had given Effie gifts of the piano, a book on botany, valuable jewelry, and fruits from his garden. He named a marriage date and then turned her away, she said. Shaw's attorney's sought to besmirch her character by producing a witness who said she lived at a place where "dashing fellows" lived. The jury deliberated and ruled in Effie's favor. Effie was awarded the one hundred thousand dollars she requested.

Shaw appealed. The next trial, in March 1860, made national news. Shaw's lawyers put forth a case that Effie had sought out Shaw to entrap him. Depositions from men in Brooklyn, Cincinnati, and Charleston said she was a prostitute. Judge Sam Reber wouldn't allow testimony that disputed those contentions. The second verdict went to Shaw, and he kept his one hundred thousand dollars. The court turned down Effie's request for another trial on the basis that some of the jurors were prejudiced. As far as the court was concerned, she was the nineteenth-century equivalent of the woman who fakes a neck injury in a car crash to get money out of the other driver.

The outcome left one question unanswered: Had Effie won, how would it have affected Shaw's plans for his botanical garden? He had amassed a fortune of $250,000 when he retired in 1839. Losing to Effie would have sucked nearly half that amount out of Shaw's pocket. Botanical Garden Archivist Andy Colligan believes a verdict against Shaw may have postponed some of the development of the grounds and the buildings. He cautions that it's all speculation, but it's a worthy question because it concerns a woman who was either a gold digger or a bride jilted at the altar.

The Light Side of Schools

Like many youngsters, William Ittner hated going to school. But almost alone among that group, Ittner was able to change what he hated about getting an education in St. Louis schools after the Civil War. Born in 1864, he detested the dark buildings of the city schools, especially their hallways. They lacked indoor plumbing, there were too few exits, and basement classrooms were dirty. He thought they were prisons.

The son of a prominent businessman and congressman, Ittner grew up to be an architect whose work included high-end homes in Compton Heights and Fox Park. He might have kept designing fine homes if a new office hadn't opened up on the St. Louis Board of Education. He was elected the board's Commissioner of School Buildings in 1897.

It was a time of explosive growth, in an era when the leadership of the city schools was progressive. Ittner designed forty-nine schools for the city, but not just any schools. He opened up the buildings and allowed light to bathe the interiors, even the basements. His floor plans were such that corridors had windows on the sides and not just on the ends. That eliminated the darkened hallways. He took advantage of generous budgets to put up buildings that would still be gems a century later. Today, the South Side is filled with those architectural jewels. A list of those South Side schools includes names like Cleveland, Fanning, Gardenville, McKinley, Mullanphy, and Oak Hill.

Ittner resigned as commissioner in 1910 and remained as "consulting architect" to the board until 1914. He went on to design hundreds of school buildings throughout the country and see his ideas become a standard for school architecture. Before he died in 1936 he designed the Missouri Athletic Club in 1916, the Scottish Rite Cathedral in 1921, and the Continental Building in 1929.

Today, the firms of William B. Ittner, Inc., and Ittner & Bowersox, Inc., carry his namesake. Many school buildings throughout the city and the country carry his legacy. In recent years, the St. Louis Public Schools have targeted many of the local ones for closing. Those who have protested have done so not only because the buildings are old, but because they are beautiful and lift the spirit. It's a fitting tribute to someone who sought to bring light to the dark parts of a student's day.

The Man Behind St. Louis Hills

In much of the rest of the South Side, it's common to have a mix of houses, stores, building materials, and building styles. Frame homes often are next to brick corner stores. But in St. Louis Hills, consistency is the norm. Almost every home and apartment is solid brick. There are no stores or offices off the primary thoroughfares. Even the schools, churches, and parks match the rest of the neighborhood.

The man responsible for that consistent appearance is Cyrus Crane Willmore. After developing homes in Normandy, University City, and Webster Groves in the county and Kingshighway Hills in St. Louis in the early 1920s, he decided seven hundred acres of dairy farmland in St. Louis's southwest corner were ready for development. Already, the property had a history. David R. Francis, who is best known as the president of the 1904 World's Fair, bought it in 1884. In 1916, Francis donated sixty acres of the land for Francis Park.

Willmore started laying out Francis's former property just before the start of the Great Depression. The Depression could have given him reason to allow contractors who bought his land to do shoddy work that would bring prices down, but he insisted on exceptionally high standards of workmanship and architecture through the economic squeeze that threatened to break him. To bring a variety of income levels, he provided space for apartments, duplexes, small homes, and high-end homes, as well as schools and churches. To add to the neighborhood, he donated seventy acres of his land for Willmore Park in 1946. The project continued for several years after Willmore died in 1949. St. Louis Hills Estates, which was finished in the 1950s, features ranch homes instead of the two-story houses in the original development.

Willmore's plan for an area with quality homes and "country living in the city" became a reality. St. Louis Hills has grown into a premier neighborhood for the St. Louis metropolitan area. For this, South Siders can thank a man who insisted on maintaining the highest standards at the risk of his own personal fortune.

Cyrus Willmore, second from left, poses with dignitaries outside his office in St. Louis Hills

When Dagwood Went To McKinley

For eight decades, one of the most popular and consistently funny comic strips has been a tale of family life, keeping ahead of the boss, and the pursuit of the world's biggest sandwich. The comic is "Blondie," and its themes can be traced back more than ninety years to McKinley High School when creator Murat Bernard "Chic" Young attended the school.

Young showed that budding talent in cartoons he created from 1915 to 1919 for McKinley's *Carnation*, a publication that looked like a yearbook, except that it came out twice a year. His style wasn't much different from the "Blondie" cartoons that first appeared in 1930. One, titled "Vacations," shows campers, a man hurriedly eating in the best Dagwood fashion, and a student pulling weeds in the Missouri Botanical Garden. To the student picking weeds, a man shouts, "Hey, you're pickin' our valuable prune plant." Another cartoon shows McKinley battling Soldan High School in debate and football. "McKinley nearly talks Soldan's ears off in a debate," one panel says. In another panel, a player kicks a field goal from the 40-yard line. "Oh, isn't he cute," somebody says from

the stands. And for those who think Young only could draw, he was also librarian of the McKinley Literary Society. The experience he gained at McKinley made the efforts of Dagwood to take uninterrupted naps even funnier and were among the steps he took to make "Blondie" one of the most popular strips ever.

After Young's death in 1973, his son, Dean Young, and John Marshall took over the strip. Today, "Blondie" appears in more than two thousand newspapers around the world. Perhaps remembering the influence of those McKinley High School days, Dean Young drew a cartoon in 2004 for McKinley's centennial. As Dagwood holds a huge sandwich with candles on top, Blondie says, "Dagwood made this in honor of the McKinley High School Centennial Celebration in 2004."

If anyone had asked Dagwood "the St. Louis question" about where he went to high school, he might have answered, "I'm a McKinley Goldbug."

Betty Grable, South Side Gal

World War II pinup girl Betty Grable is remembered locally with a star on the St. Louis Walk of Fame at 6350 Delmar Avenue, but the star could just as easily have been at the spot near where she lived at 3858 Lafayette Avenue after she was born in 1916. That house and the surrounding houses on the south side of Lafayette were demolished to make way for Interstate 44. The star could have been in front of the nearby Mullanphy School at 4221 Shaw Boulevard, where she first attended school. Or it could have been at her first church, St. John's Episcopal, at 3664 Arsenal Street. The Reverend Killian Stimpson baptized her at the church on March 26, 1921. Church records say her sponsors included two aunts, Estelle and Rebecca Grable. Susan Rehkopf, archivist of the Episcopal Diocese of Missouri, recalls her father telling her she was baptized in the same font as Betty Grable. That font is still in use. Wags at the church call it the "Grable font."

Wherever it's best to remember Grable in St. Louis, part of her remained a South Sider long after she left the area for Hollywood. Pushed by her mother, Lillian Grable, Betty learned acting and dancing and started making vaudeville appearances. In the late 1920s, she moved with her mother to Hollywood. Her father, Conn, stayed behind, and Conn and Lillian eventually divorced. Betty appeared in her first film in 1929 and signed a contract with Samuel Goldwyn the next year. She was so popular that pinup pictures of her were carried by soldiers, sailors, and Marines everywhere during World War II. Altogether, she acted in sixty-one films into the 1950s, including *Million Dollar Legs* in 1939 and *How to Marry a Millionaire* in 1953.

One of her last appearances was at the Muny Opera in 1971 in *This Is Show Business* with Don Ameche and Rudy Vallee. After she died of cancer two years later, an obituary in the *Post-Dispatch* said that when she returned to St. Louis in the 1930s to visit her father, she would stop by the home of her aunts at 4118 Juniata Street. "They have coffee every day, and there's sure to be something good to eat," she said. The two-story brick home still has a generous covered front porch and is down the street from Mann School.

Joe and Yogi

It started with not-so-gentle games of King of the Hill in the 5400 block of Elizabeth Avenue. Mickey and John loved to stand at the top of the hill and push their little brothers Joe and Lawrence down. "We used to try to give them a hard time," said Mickey, who was Joe's big brother. Then Joe and Lawrence grew older, picked up bats and catchers' mitts, and became kings of a much bigger hill. Joe's last name was Garagiola, and he grew up to play baseball and be a Hall of Fame baseball broadcaster. Lawrence later became known as Yogi Berra, the Hall of Fame catcher for the Yankees and a well-known speaker of creative English. They lived across the street from each other. Ben Pucci, who played for the All-American Football Conference 1948 Champion Cleveland Browns, was another of Joe and Yogi's neighbors and playmates on the block. Later on, another Hall of Famer broadcaster Jack Buck, called the block home for a while, but when people on the Hill think about the great ones from Elizabeth Avenue, they're talking about Joe and Yogi.

When Joe and Yogi were little, Elizabeth Avenue was a great place for kids to play, and there was nothing they liked doing more than playing ball. "They were two peas in a pod," Mickey said. Early on, Joe, Yogi, Ben, and others played for a team sponsored by the neighborhood's Stags Athletic Club. "They were the best ballplayers on the team, so you know they had to go somewhere," Charles Riva, who also played on the Stags team, said of Joe and Yogi. Riva lived on the same block. Mickey wound up marrying Riva's sister Adele.

"There was always something going on, all the time," Riva said. Yogi painted ten-yard lines on the street during football season so the gang could play touch football. He dropped out of school after eighth grade to work at a factory, but he was fired because he would wander off at lunch to play ball and forget to come back to work. So he played American Legion ball instead. Mickey also quit school after eighth grade to work as a waiter at the swank Ruggeri's Restaurant at 2300 Edwards Street. After Ruggeri's closed in 1985, he spent the next fourteen years as a waiter at Pietro's at 3801 Watson Road. He also gained fame locally from 1969 to 1985 by announcing on the old *Wrestling at the Chase* on KPLR Channel 11. Never mind that he didn't go to high school. Everyone knew him for his class.

Joe was one person who didn't stop school at the end of eighth grade. He played ball at St. Mary's High School and also played for the old city WPA league. The Cardinals were so impressed they gave him five hundred dollars to sign with the team. The Redbirds also wanted to sign Yogi but wouldn't give him the same five hundred-dollar bonus. So Yogi went with the Yankees. After Joe came to the majors in 1946, people on the Hill celebrated by sponsoring Joe Garagiola Night at Sportsman's Park. "It will always be a top thrill to me because that night I saw many people there like Mama and Pop—people who didn't know what baseball was but wanted to be there because 'this is one of our boys,'" he said in his 1960 book, *Baseball Is a Funny Game*. Garagiola spent nine years with the Cardinals, Pirates, Cubs, and Giants before ending with a so-so .257 lifetime average in 1954. His career took off after that, first as a Cardinals broadcaster and then as an NBC baseball commentator and personality. Since then, he's stayed close to friends on the Hill and calls Mickey every Sunday.

Meanwhile, Yogi found glory as a catcher and a manager in both leagues. He became famous for sayings like "It's déjà vu all over again." That might lead people to think he's not too smart. Mickey says it's not so. "He's not a dumb kid like they make him out to be," he said. Mickey's nephew Bruce Marren agrees. "He was never like that," said Marren, a freelance photographer and videographer who also lives in the 5400 block of Elizabeth and has seen Yogi from time to time. Yogi has friends and family here, including a niece who lives in the Berra house on Elizabeth. Marren has seen Joe Garagiola frequently through the years, including at the 2003 ceremony where his block received an honorary designation from the city as Hall of Fame Place. People on the block have welcomed those who come to see a place where so many famous athletes lived. "The neighbors are pretty friendly about tourists coming through," Marren said. During the 2009 All-Star Game here, "I thought about putting up a stand and selling photos," he said with a laugh.

A Legacy in the Ring

From the moment Devon Alexander started boxing as a teenager at the Marquette Recreation Center at 4025 Minnesota Avenue, it was clear there was something special about him. "I've always been a boxing fan. I went from fan to involvement because of Devon Alexander," said Marquette Recreation Center Director Debra Craig. If anybody hasn't heard, Alexander is the Light Welterweight Champion of the World Boxing Council and the International Boxing Federation. "His name is Alexander the Great," Craig said, putting emphasis on Alexander's accomplishments.

Alexander may have become a champ, but he hasn't forgotten his roots. When he's in town, he still trains at the center where he learned how to box as a teenager. Former World Welterweight Champion Cory Spinks also trained at Marquette before turning pro. Spinks is the son of former Heavyweight Champ Leon Spinks and nephew of former Heavyweight and Light-Heavyweight Champ Michael Spinks. Alexander and the Spinks family are part of a celebrated St. Louis boxing tradition. The local greats begin with South Side native Henry Armstrong in the 1930s, who was Featherweight, Welterweight, and Lightweight Champ and some say pound-for-pound the best boxer to enter a ring. In the 1950s, Archie Moore dominated the Light-Heavyweight division. And the 1960s witnessed Sonny Liston, who had his first win in St. Louis and was World Heavyweight Champion before Muhammad Ali defeated him in 1965.

There are many at the Marquette Recreation Center who hope to be the next Devon Alexander. Boys as young as eight learn the fundamentals in the second-floor training room at the center. Danny McGinnist, a St. Louis Sheriff's Department employee, has volunteered at Marquette for a dozen years. "You try to help the kids stay out of the street," McGinnist said.

Joseph Dunlap, a longtime coach for the boxing programs at the city's recreation centers, is now the coach at Marquette. "It keeps these young boys' minds occupied and keeps them focused on something other than the streets," he said. Boxing programs are offered at seven of the city's nine recreation centers. Boxers spar with headgear and wear mouthpieces, padded gloves, and body padding. All of that keeps them safe, he said.

Jarvis Williams is one of Dunlap's students. The 2008 Roosevelt High School graduate started training at age thirteen after his uncle's urging. The uncle is in jail and writes Williams and still pushes him to keep training. Boxing has taught him to control his anger and to stay disciplined, Williams said. "It's kept me away from the streets," Williams said. "If I didn't have boxing, honestly, I don't know where I'd be at today."

Such people need friends in high places, and they found one in Dan Kirner. Kirner was a city police officer when he saw how boxing was helping to keep young North Siders off the street. So he volunteered as a boxing announcer and judge. He kept it up after he retired as a sergeant in the early 1990s and after he became alderman in the South Side's 25th Ward in 1999. "He said it was like a marvel. They didn't do drugs because they would be thrown out of boxing," said Kirner's wife, Dorothy. She became 25th Ward alderwoman after Dan died in 2003 and kept the job until 2009. She shied away from boxing but became a judge after her husband persuaded her to take another look. She and Dan knew Devon Alexander, Cory Spinks, and others when they trained at Marquette. She also recalled how Dan killed a plan to save money by dropping the boxing program from the city's recreation centers. If he'd written the headline, it would have been, "Kirner Scores a Knockout for the Kids."

The South Side's Foot-Stompin', Holy Ghost Singin', Gospel Playin' Duo

On May 21, 1927, a doctor paid a call to deliver a baby in Datto, Arkansas. The boy's parents couldn't pay cash, so they gave him three-dozen eggs and a red rooster. As the boy grew, he learned to give up his shoes every May 15 so they would stay in good shape for cold weather. As poor as he was, he found $7.50 when he was fourteen to buy a piano. Then Almus "Slim" Cox taught himself to play.

"I learned myself how to play that piano. I never had a lesson," Cox said, as he belted out a tune on an electric piano in a radio and recording studio in the back of his crowded Slim and Zella Mae Cox Furniture Store at 2831 Chippewa Street. He doesn't mind that he never learned to read notes. It's more important that he play country gospel like his favorites, Jerry Lee Lewis, Jimmy Swaggart, and the country gospel musician Howard Goodman. If he just read the notes in a service, everybody in church would fall asleep, he said. "That's why Slim and Zella Mae can get up in those telethons and get the phones ringing," Slim said in the booming voice that watchers of the telethons and other programs on KNLC-Channel 24 know so well. Slim's piano playing and the singing of his wife, Zella Mae, are familiar to viewers of KNLC, as well as seven low-powered television stations and thirteen radio stations operated by Larry Rice's New Life Evangelistic Center.

The music also is familiar to listeners of Miroslaw Desperak's hillbilly country program on Catholic radio station FIAT 94.7 FM in Czestochowa, Poland. Slim and Zella Mae's song "Walking My Lord Up Calvary Hill" was one of the station's biggest hits at the start of 2010. Slim and Zella Mae recorded it in the 1960s, and it has been enjoying a second life of sorts. It zoomed in popularity around the world in 2004 and again in 2010, where it raced up the worldwide country gospel chart. It has been hot in Australia, Denmark, Canada, and England and in numerous states in the United States. "It makes me feel thrilled to know we're getting to people," Slim said. The Coxes also have their share of fans locally. "I love the old foot-stomping tongues of fire

gospel," said Ridgley "Hound-
dog" Brown, who dropped
in to Cox's furniture store
one Saturday to say hello to
Slim and Zella Mae. "He is
a terrific piano player," said
Brown, a retiree who does
programming for KDHX 88.1
FM. "He plays it like a barrel house piano style."

Cox honed his style playing in bands and then with Zella Mae after they got
married in 1948. When she was born on October 23, 1930, in Mammoth
Springs, Arkansas, her parents didn't have to give up three dozen eggs. Her
father, a Pentecostal preacher, delivered her. Slim maintains he found out
he really loved Zella Mae when he discovered she could pick 360 pounds of
cotton a day. After they married, they sang on small radio stations in northern Arkansas and southern Missouri. They continued performing on the
radio after he moved to Wellston in the late 1950s and worked for Schweig
Engel Furniture. After twelve years at Schweig Engel, Cox started his furniture company at its present location. In the meantime, Slim and Zella Mae
continued the musical work that people know them by today. In the morning
before school, they recorded a fifteen-minute show at home. Cox then took
the tape to KXEN Radio. They also recorded sixteen different albums and
went around the country on an old Greyhound bus. "It was very exciting and
sometimes very tiring," said their daughter Sharon Hardcastle, of O'Fallon,
Missouri, recalling those days on the road. "I've been singing ever since I can
remember." Another daughter, Brenda Chitty, of O'Fallon, Missouri, said, "It
was like spinning in a circle around and around."

In recent years, Slim and Zella Mae have limited their performing to Larry
Rice's radio and television stations, a radio show from 6 to 7 a.m. Saturdays
on WEW 770, and an annual performance at Kirkwood's Green Tree Festival in September. But they stay active in the community. He was president of
the Chippewa Broadway Business Association for seven years and is president
of the Chippewa Neighborhood Association. "South St. Louis has been good
to us," said Cox. He also credits his faith for what he's become. "We need to
preach about a hell to shun and a heaven to gain," he said. It's not bad for
somebody who cost his parents thirty-six eggs and a rooster.

Photographing St. Louis

Robert Arteaga and his sons, Wayne and Eldon, are best known for their efforts to photograph the building of the Gateway Arch. The elder Arteaga had a contract to take four official photographs of the Arch during each month of its construction, but he went overboard. Robert, Wayne, and Eldon made about twelve thousand images of the Arch during the two-and-a-half-year construction process. It's the most extensive set taken of the monument's construction.

The Arteagas also were busy elsewhere and captured many South Side moments on film. Bob took aerial pictures of the construction of Hampton Village after World War II and of Kingshighway Boulevard and Chippewa Street before construction started on Southtown Famous. He also took pictures of car dealerships on South Kingshighway in the 1940s. Eldon took pictures for the Teamsters Union on the South Side. That work was done from offices downtown and then on the North Side until the Arteagas moved to a building in the South Side's Southampton neighborhood in 1972. Today, Eldon and his son, Brad, carry on the family tradition at that location. Besides taking pictures, Brad is active in the community as president of the Southtown Business Association and the St. Louis Hills Neighborhood Association.

Eldon and Brad are proud of their collection of negatives, which numbers over a million. They are especially proud of the Arch photos. Bob was passionate about the Gateway Arch from the moment he heard about it. Even before the government officially decided the Arch would go up on the site of the new Jefferson National Expansion Memorial, Robert put it on the logo for his photo shop at 19 S. Third Street. When President Harry Truman walked by the store during a visit to dedicate the expansion memorial grounds in 1950, he asked, "What idiot put this sign over here? The arch isn't even okayed yet." Arteaga piped back, "I'm that idiot," and Truman laughed.

Brad was sixteen when his grandfather died in 1982. That's old enough to absorb Robert's stories of that meeting with Truman, along with his tales of taking pictures of the likes of Lou Gehrig, Babe Ruth, and a rookie named Stan Musial. Brad still hears stories from his father about snapping pictures at the top of the Arch. Until his uncle Wayne died in 2009, he heard more stories from him. Brad followed his father and grandfather around when they took pictures. When Brad was in second grade, he knew what he wanted to do. So did Robert after he first started taking pictures.

Born in 1903, Robert was fascinated by what happened when he took a picture of a moving train. "You could freeze something in an instant, and it stays that way, but you keep going," said Eldon. In 1930, he got a job working for a man who had the contract to take pictures of the St. Louis Cardinals and Browns. Robert's scorecard of Stan Musial's first game included the penciled-in observation, "Musial has my OK." Robert got tired of his boss getting the credit for his work and went on his own in 1946. Robert's interest in the Arch led him to get the contract to take pictures of the construction there. Eldon remembers how he climbed a ladder on his trips to take pictures until the Arch reached ninety feet. He soon started taking freelance pictures of people working on the Arch. This was exciting, but nothing like the excitement of taking pictures on October 28, 1965, when the last piece was put in the Arch. "When that National Anthem started, you could just feel that tremendous pride for St. Louis," Eldon said.

Today, Eldon and Brad specialize in aerial, architectural, and product photography. Brad carried on his family's tradition of sports photos by taking aerial photos of Busch Stadium on opening day. Those photos—both digital and film—convince Brad that film remains better. "Digital has a long way to go to compete with film," Brad said. But he takes digital because that's what people want. "Digital has made this a 'That's good enough' society," Brad said. Brad's not interested in anything that's "good enough," and neither were his father, uncle, and grandfather. If they emulate anybody, it's the people who built the Arch. Maybe that's why there's still a picture of the Arch on the company logo.

Everybody Knows Mickey McTague

All of nine, Marshall E. McTague Jr. sat at Kiel Auditorium and heard Harry Truman belittle those who didn't think he had a chance in the 1948 presidential election. His father, Marshall E. McTague Sr., narrowly lost a bid for Congress four years before. In the 1950s, he'd be groomed to run for governor, but for now, he was one more person in the welcoming committee. "I remember Truman holding up the *Post-Dispatch* with scorn because they didn't endorse him," Marshall Jr. said. He also remembers shaking Harry's hand. Like his father, he goes by Mickey. It was one of the first memories in a lifetime of collecting memories of important people he has met.

Mickey related the story one Saturday afternoon at Shaw Coffee at Marconi and Shaw avenues on the Hill. He wore a dark green ivy cap, a herringbone jacket, a gray sweater, blue shirt, and green T-shirt. Over three hours, he spoke about the politicians and famous people he's known and worked for: Bob Hope, Lenny Bruce, Mayor Al Cervantes, Mayor Ray Tucker, Joe Garagiola, and Thomas Eagleton are on the list. He has pictures posing with many of them on the wall of his apartment at Donovan and Lansdowne avenues in St. Louis Hills.

He spoke as well about how he lost his father at an early age. Three days after his son graduated from eighth grade, forty-seven-year-old Marshall E. McTague Sr. dropped dead of a heart attack. After that, Mickey's mother almost died of tuberculosis. Mickey took over as the titular leader of his family at 3128 Allen Avenue. Although the senior McTague had bought enough insurance to give his six children a good living, grief weighed heavily on Mickey.

The St. Mary's High School graduate, however, found a way out through comedy writing. As he moved into adulthood, big-name comedians started noticing. He wrote material for Lenny Bruce when he appeared one night in the mid-1960s at the Crystal Palace in Gaslight Square. Bruce gave him $200. Garagiola gave him $250 for a monologue at the 1965 Baseball Writers Dinner at the Jefferson Hotel downtown. But Mickey's biggest connection was with Bob Hope. Mickey met Hope in 1958 when he was performing at the Muny Opera and wrote topical material for the legendary comedian whenever he was in the area. After Hope died at the age of one hundred in 2003, Mickey was at the private funeral Mass. An early check he received from Hope, for five hundred dollars, was to write some jokes for the Academy Awards in 1966. Over the years, he's seen the change in comedy long enough to be able to make this observation: "Humor has become so mean-spirited, leaving almost nothing to the imagination, with a lot of spite in it." He might have gone elsewhere to be a big comedy writer, but he decided to stay on the South Side.

For most of his life, Mickey toiled for the city. He worked off and on for the city from 1959 to 1971, when he stayed on until he retired in 2007. By being in patronage jobs for the city collector of revenue, license collector, and sheriff's office, he was able to do work for mayors, including Ray Tucker and A. J. Cervantes. He is also close to Francis R. Slay, father of Mayor Francis G. Slay. Once in a while, he used to stop by the bar of the 11th Ward Alderman Albert "Red" Villa. He liked the cigar smoking of the legendary 7th Ward Alderman Ray Leisure. He's shared memories with the late Senator Thomas Eagleton and the late Governor Mel Carnahan. Since Mickey retired, he's been working on a screenplay about Bob Hope, Bing Crosby, and others coming back from the dead for a few days. The memories he shared of Hope are among the ones he has collected in a lifetime of knowing countless people. Everybody knows Mickey McTague, because Mickey McTague knows everybody.

Making It Right on South Kingshighway

The cop was aghast. A car dealer had asked for the keys to a customer's car so he could take it out and appraise it for a trade-in. As the story is told now, the dealer threw the keys up on his roof and told the customer he'd have to buy the car he was looking at or walk home. The customer went to the cop for help. When the cop demanded the keys back, the dealer said it was a civil matter and told him to stay out of it. The cop sent a paddy wagon around to pick up everybody at the dealership for stealing the keys. Word got around about what Officer Dave Sinclair had done at the North Side dealership, and the widespread practice stopped. Years later, when Sinclair's first dealerships opened on South Kingshighway Boulevard early in 1966, he determined nothing like that would happen there. In the six years he operated on Kingshighway, he developed a reputation for honest dealings and hokey TV ads that made him a regional icon. In a business known for its crooks, when Sinclair died in 2009, everybody remembered him as the guy you told your grandmother to see about a car.

Sinclair started making that reputation in the midst of a crowded strip of auto stores. You could buy anything on South Kingshighway: Pontiac, Cadillac, Dodge, Lincoln, or Oldsmobile. In 1969, car dealers had twenty-one addresses from Southtown Famous north to Arsenal Street. They included such names as Vincel Pontiac, King Dodge, and Bender Best Lincoln Mercury. Add in McMahon Ford at Gravois Avenue and Chippewa Street and Placke Chevrolet and Christopher-Southwest Motor Sales Used Cars at Southwest Avenue and Kingshighway, and the number grew to an even two dozen. Sinclair had three of those addresses on either side of Tholozan Avenue on the east side of Kingshighway. Dave Sin-

clair Ford Used Cars was on the north side of Tholozan, and Dave Sinclair
Ford, Inc., and Dave Sinclair Ford Truck, Inc., were on the south side.

Dan Sinclair remembers those days. A lawyer and accountant who ran
some of Sinclair's car dealerships, he's the oldest of Dave's seven children.
"South Kingshighway was at the time the Manchester and South Lindbergh of now," Dan claimed. But he wasn't as impressed about the buildings and lots themselves. "It was small and old and antiquated." For all of
this, Sinclair moved cars, in part with a familiar bet of a free undercoat
if anybody beat his deals. He had been making this offer since he quit the
city police in 1956 and started as a car salesman. By the mid-1960s,
Ford offered to help set up Sinclair with his own business.

Not long after he opened, Dave Sinclair became a pioneer in local advertising by buying his own thirty-second spots on KPLR-TV Channel 11.
"It was very primitive by today's standards," Dan said. The first one showed
white-gloved hands on a black background dealing cards that said "For
a great deal, come to Dave Sinclair." Later, he read his own copy behind
a podium, as he did the rest of his life. People liked the ads, Dan said.
"The customers felt like there was a personal emotional attachment. He
was talking to *you*, not the masses of people. He was frequently quoted as
saying he didn't want anybody to be unhappy that had done business with
Dave Sinclair." And Dave didn't forget his roots. "He was a city policeman, and his father and uncles had been St. Louis city police officers,"
Dan said. "As soon as he got his own place, he started hiring ex-city po-
licemen." Maybe forty or fifty city police officers eventually came to work
for him. As an ex-cop, he kept his police revolver. He had it with him
when he and others stayed overnight to catch a thief who'd been stealing
cars from his lot. When the robber showed up, Sinclair used the revolver
to keep him at bay until police came to take the crook away.

If Sinclair had gotten his wish, he would have stayed on Kingshighway.
That's where his customers were, Dan said. But the place was too small.
His used cars were stashed on lots for blocks around. "Ford Motor Co.
convinced him to move. He did not want to move," his son said. Finally,
he decided to move to 7466 South Lindbergh Boulevard. It's one of four
dealerships the Sinclairs have today. The customers followed. Then as
now, they knew if the car wasn't right, Dave Sinclair would make it right.

Don't Be Confused

In hindsight, it probably wasn't a good idea, but then again, it did sell a lot of washers and dryers. As the cameras rolled at the Channel 11 studio, Steve Mizerany poured wood alcohol on top of a washer and set it on fire. "I was showing somebody it won't catch on fire," the master hawker remembered. But then some of the alcohol dripped down and caught some rubber on fire. Soon a backdrop curtain was ablaze. "The fire department had to come and put it out," Mizerany said. "It got a lot of play." For Mizerany, whose crazy antics and ads for his appliance stores were fixtures on local television stations from the 1950s until he retired in 1990, it was just another ad, and it all started on the South Side.

Mizerany is now in his late eighties. He gets around on a wheelchair at the Bethesda Meadows Nursing Home in Ellisville, but he's still eager to talk about how everything started with his father's grocery store at 10th Street and Park Avenue. He attended St. Vincent de Paul School not far from his house and then McKinley High School. Like everybody else in this Lebanese family, Mizerany helped out at the grocery store. "I didn't learn to sell. I was friendly," Mizerany said. Then his brother Joe started the first Mizerany appliance store at 3849 S. Broadway after World War II. Friends and family helped out, including Joe Farhatt, a childhood buddy who would follow him through his career. Steve was out on the floor, hamming it up. "I always was a silly guy. I was sort of a nitwit," he said. He loved the Germans of South St. Louis. "They always bought from us," he said. "They're good people, the Germans." Soon, the Mizerany family opened a second store at 18th Street and Geyer Avenue. Then stores opened in Maplewood and Pine Lawn. Eventually, there were twenty-four such stores.

THE DECENT BOYS

The ads were a big part of this increase. "I wasn't serious at all. It was 'act silly,'" Mizerany said. "Our commercials were so bad that the people liked 'em and bought." His son Vince explains the thinking this way: "The idea was to get people's attention on television." That got them into the store, where salesmen made the sale. He wasn't just silly on television, either. Vince said, "He was a riot to live with. Everywhere he went, he'd act silly."

Eventually, Farhatt and Steve broke away from others in the original Mizerany stores and formed Mizerany New Deal. In time, there were seven Mizerany New Deal stores, including one near the Bevo Mill at 4719 Gravois Avenue. And the ads continued. "His ad used to say, 'The Bevo Mill is next to us,'" said a volunteer at Bethesda Meadows, Bob Morris. To show Mizerany's prices were the lowest, he introduced a famous line, "Don't be confused. We don't bait and switch." He was on the radio with Jack Buck and worked with the famous announcer in the Celebrities Against Police softball fund-raiser at Fox Park at Shenandoah and Ohio avenues for the St. Louis Police Relief Association. The benefit raised about ten thousand dollars. He also became known for a routine in which he zoomed through his store in roller skates. These antics brought him considerable success. But, he said, "All that was an accident. It's not that I'm smart." Indeed, he succeeded in selling some people washers and dryers, but he made everybody laugh.

The Nightmares Linger

The smile Sadik Kukic shows to customers of his Bevo Mill neighborhood restaurant conceals a darker reality. Too often, he awakens in a sweat. He's had another nightmare about the five months he spent in two Serbian concentration camps for the crime of being Muslim. He came from Bosnia to St. Louis in 1993 to escape an ethnic war following the breakup of Yugoslavia. About 250,000 people died and more than 3 million became refugees from 1992 to 1995. Tens of thousands of refugees like Kukic came to the South Side, bringing new vitality to an area centered in the Bevo Mill neighborhood. One of the earliest of those refugees, Kukic became a leader of the city's Bosnian community and the owner of one of the best Bosnian restaurants in St. Louis. Often, he will laugh about old times before the war with other Bosnians who come to his Taft Street Restaurant and Bar at 4457 Gravois Road, but the dreaded memories continue. If he's hiding the pain, he knows that many of his customers also are disguising anguish over what happened to them. "Some of us admit it. Some of us don't," Kukic said in his kitchen, while he prepared two rib-eye steaks.

For Kukic, who was born in 1965, the story began when he went to work for about seven years as a chef on boats traveling from the former Yugoslavia to Germany. Then the war broke out, and he came back to his hometown of Brezovo Polje in Bosnia. "I wasn't politically involved in anything," he said. One day, Serbs rounded up the men and brought them to a concentration camp. After twenty-three days, he was taken to another concentration camp, where he stayed for about four months. "They beat me, they didn't feed me, and I did what needed to be done," Kukic said. He weighed about 220 pounds when he came in and about 97 pounds when he left. "Every day there was different torture," Kukic said. "I was sleeping five months on a concrete floor. Sometimes they fed us, sometimes they didn't," he said. But then his old employer in Belgrade did a work of mercy. He said he needed the help of Kukic and fifteen others. "He was doing us a favor," Kukic said. "I can't forget him for the rest of my life." Kukic spent ten months working in Belgrade before the International Institute brought him to St. Louis along with his wife, Edina, his son, Emir, who is now twenty-one, and his brother, Ekrem.

Kukic was out of danger but still had to struggle. Broke and not knowing any English, he took a factory job and then a job at a taco place. "I didn't speak any English, and all recipes were in Spanish," he said. After he got a car in 1994, he moved up to a catering place and then to the St. Louis Club in Clayton. "Money was OK, but it was very good to have that kind of place on your resume," Kukic said. He learned English from his time in the kitchen, by studying at home, and six months of classes at the International Institute. In 2000, he opened his first restaurant, the Gulf Coast, at 3191 South Grand Boulevard. Then in 2002, he had a bout with cancer, which was cured when a kidney was removed. In March 2005, he opened Taft Street Restaurant and closed the Gulf Coast four months later. In four of the five years since then, the *Riverfront Times* has listed Taft Street Restaurant as the best Bosnian cuisine. Meanwhile, he served three years as president of the Bosnian Chamber of Commerce and was founder of the annual Bosnian Festival for the area.

He seemed the picture of the successful refugee immigrant, but his struggles continued. "Sometimes, these things come to you and leave you for a while," he said. But there are joys, including the time he spends with his daughter, Lajla, who is three. There also is his sense of thankfulness for being in America. "I consider St. Louis a good place to start for newcomers. And I deeply believe that the United States is a country of opportunity." Several years ago, heading back to the United States from a vacation trip to Bosnia, he thought, "We are coming home. We are coming home."

Bucket Joe: Happily Off the Street

Like the stories of Wyatt Earp and Jesse James, the legend of Bucket Joe has grown over time, but Joe wasn't a lawman or an outlaw, only a homeless man on the South Side whom everybody seemed to know. He walked along Grand Boulevard and Gravois Avenue carrying a bucket he used to make money by washing windows. Some people remember him swinging at passing cars with an old broom at Chippewa Street and Gravois Avenue. Some yelled at Joe in derision, some in friendship. He hasn't been on the streets for years, and it would be easy to say somebody made up the stories about him, if it wasn't for the fact that so many people remember him.

Bucket Joe was and is a real person with a real name. He didn't disappear or simply go away; rather, he found a home. In an August 29, 1990, article, *South Side Journal* reporter Lois Kendall said Joseph "Bucket Joe" Mossberger had been living on the streets since he was eighteen in the early 1960s. "He lumbered up and down the sidewalks of the South Side for some thirty years, a big man with a shaved head and a loping gait. He wore raggedy dress pants chopped off at the knees and scuffed brogan shoes without socks. He rarely wore a jacket, except on the coldest days. And in either hand, he carried buckets." Home was an empty building or an alley. He ate what strangers fed him or what he found in garbage cans. "He'd been hit by cars, arrested by police and incarcerated in mental institutions," Kendall wrote. Then he disappeared, which led to speculation that something terrible had happened to him.

But Kendall had good news to report. He was living in a six-family flat on the South Side and receiving Social Security checks. He was sleeping in a real bed and eating regularly. He'd allowed a reporter to speak to him so those he had known on the street would know he was all right. Now sixty-six, he is still doing well and living in an apartment, said Clifford Cockrell, a landlord and Forest Park Southeast resident who has known Mossberger all his life. Cockrell got tired of seeing Mossberger on the streets and got him off. "He's very happy. He eats three meals a day," Cockrell said.

Mossberger, who is developmentally disabled, hasn't had a drink in twenty years, Cockrell said. He has two cats and likes AM radio. He has a cake every birthday. Ever protective, Cockrell refused to allow another reporter to speak with Mossberger.

Most don't know about this happy ending to a story that didn't start well, but speculation and memories remain, including in a public Facebook page put up by the website www.southcitystl. Don L. O'Toole Jr., who now lives in Louisiana, wrote on the Facebook page that he made friends with Joe as a youngster selling newspapers in front of the White Castle at Grand and Gravois. "He was the source of lots of fun and dare I say entertainment," he wrote. "Hopefully, he is doing as well as he was when this article came out." Others who wrote on the page recalled hearing that he got the name "Bucket Joe" because he carried a beer bucket around. Another remembered giving Joe a gallon of Kool-Aid when he was playing roller hockey behind the Oak Hill School at Morgan Ford Road and Osceola Street one summer. One more recounted how Mossberger wandered into Mass late at St. Mary Magdalen, 4611 Sutherland Avenue, when the priest was finishing giving out communion. He wandered up to the front and waited until the priest came back down and served him communion. Mossberger left, and the priest never mentioned it again.

Many of the senior citizens at the Five Star Senior Center at 2832 Arsenal Street may be uncomfortable about getting on Facebook, but they have plenty of memories of Bucket Joe. "I remember seeing him walk up and down the Gravois-Grand area carrying his white milk jug," said Mike Howard, who manages the center. Doloras Morfia, one of the senior citizens at the center, recalled that Mossberger ate sometimes at a feeding program at St. Vincent de Paul Church, 1408 S. 10th Street. "I've heard stories that he was all right, that he moved into an apartment," said Billy Watkins, another senior citizen at Five Star. At the clubhouse of the Gateway Corkball Club on Walsh Street east of Ulena Avenue, Marty Kirner recalled seeing Mossberger years ago at Amberg Field in the Dutchtown neighborhood. "He'd walk all over South St. Louis. He was homeless before homeless was popular," Kirner said. Everybody saw him and everybody realized the need, but thanks to one person who decided to fill that need, Mossberger today is off the streets.

Holding Court at a Bar

Alderman Albert "Red" Villa didn't bother meeting constituents in a fancy office at City Hall. He didn't even have a fancy office in his 11th Ward, which covers most of the Carondelet neighborhood at the southern end of the city. A constituent who wanted a job, a pothole fixed, or trash picked up headed to Table No. 1 at The Cottage, a saloon Villa operated at 8129 S. Broadway. The complaint would be resolved over a cold Bud, while Red puffed away at his ever-present stogie. Several times a week, Villa headed to City Hall to take care of the problems he'd discussed at The Cottage. That was the way it was with Villa, who remarked that his political base was his saloon.

Villa operated the saloon from 1931 to 1977. For two years before the end of Prohibition, the saloon technically wasn't legal. He co-owned two taverns before he purchased The Cottage with fellow politician Jimmy McAteer. Twice during Prohibition he was convicted of misdemeanor bootlegging violations.

After he was elected to the Board of Aldermen in 1953, Villa was known for being a gentleman and for always working for his constituents. He didn't always go along with others on the board. He once refused to take a twenty-five hundred-dollar-a-year raise and chose instead to use the money for lights at baseball fields in Carondelet Park. That didn't mean things always went smoothly for him. In 1967, he quit the board to avoid a suit brought by the Circuit Attorney's Office because he lived outside the ward at 3841 Holly Hills Boulevard, in the 13th Ward. By the time he resigned, he had moved into the 11th Ward, to 510 Dover Place. The Board of Aldermen quickly voted to reinstate Villa. He put a sign in front of the house that stated "Red Villa Lives Here."

Villa lived to see his son Thomas serve in the state legislature from 1974 to 1984 and then be elected president of the Board of Aldermen in 1987. Red was thrilled to see his son pound the gavel at meetings. But it didn't last. Red died of cancer on December 7, 1990, at his home on Dover Place. He had lived long enough to see the Board of Aldermen name its chamber after him and a bust of him holding a cigar dedicated at Virginia Avenue at Ivory Street.

Thomas made an unsuccessful run for mayor in 1993 and served as aldermanic president until 1995. He later served another tenure on the state legislature, from 2001 to 2009. At the Board of Aldermen, though, there wasn't a Villa for two years after 1995. But in 1997, Matt Villa, Tom's nephew and Red's grandson, was elected alderman in the 11th Ward. Once again, a Villa was listening to constituents' complaints, but not always at a table in a bar.

Alderman Albert (Red) Villa

A devoted public servant to the City of St. Louis and especially dedicated to the · Carondelet Community and the 11th Ward

Creating a Neighborhood Association

Rita Ford figured she would be successful if fifteen people showed up at the first meeting of a new neighborhood association for the Gravois Park neighborhood. When about seventy-five came to that first meeting in September 1999, she realized the organization could do even more than she first thought. Today, the Gravois Park Neighborhood Association is a force in the neighborhood roughly bounded by Chippewa Street, Jefferson Avenue, Cherokee Street, and Grand Boulevard. The association also is known in City Hall and throughout the city as one of the more successful St. Louis neighborhood organizations.

Neighborhood associations establish themselves either in one of the seventy-nine neighborhoods officially recognized by the city or in a different geographical area that citizens recognize. Depending on where they are, they might organize house tours, demand more police protection in areas hard hit by crime, or protest a planned housing development. The Shaw Neighborhood Improvement Association organized its annual art fair, the Lafayette Square Restoration Committee was key to the turnaround of the area around Lafayette Park, and the St. Louis Hills Neighborhood Association organized an extensive block captain program. Whatever the associations emphasize, the mayor makes a point of dropping in to their meetings on occasion. So do aldermen and other community leaders, because they know that's where they'll find those most passionate about their neighborhoods.

In Gravois Park, the group these civic leaders seek out had its start in 1987, when Ford bought a house in the neighborhood. Ford, who works in sales in the heating, ventilation, and air-conditioning industry, didn't consider herself active in the neighborhood before she purchased her house, but after she lived in Gravois Park for a few years the Sumner High School graduate noticed there were fewer homes occupied by owners and more by renters. She wanted to ensure that the condition of the neighborhood didn't decline. So in 1997, she became a block captain, responsible for making sure people in her neighborhood knew about the resources available from the city. "We had a good participation from my block." From that grew a desire to form a group for the whole neighborhood. So she passed out fliers for a first meeting at

Froebel Elementary School at 3709 Nebraska Avenue and hoped for a good crowd.

The turnout delighted her. "I learned that we did have a lot of people in the neighborhood that actually had the same dream I had for the neighborhood," Ford said. The group set goals of keeping children occupied after school, establishing a task force to deal with trash problems, and increasing home ownership. Over time, the association developed a program to keep after judges when it comes time to grant probation to people convicted of crimes in Gravois Park. The Gravois Park Justice System works with the Circuit Attorney's Office, keeps track of court dates, and sends people to probation hearings. At times, the Gravois Park Justice System has gotten judges to order parolees to stay out of the neighborhood. In another program—the Neighborhood Accountability Board—juveniles who have committed minor offenses appear before neighborhood residents sworn in by a judge to work out appropriate recompense. It could be an apology to the victim, attending an anger management class, or doing community work. Those who don't fulfill the recommendations go before juvenile authorities.

Other projects include cleaning up a block or keeping a garden. The group received keyboards and guitars for after-school programs and rakes, lawn mowers, and other tools from the Annie E. Casey Foundation. Those and other projects occupy much of the time at the association's meetings at 6 p.m. the second Tuesday of each month at St. Matthew United Church of Christ, 2613 Potomac Street. About forty to fifty people attend, including Kay Orzada, who moved to Gravois Park from Chicago in 2004. "They've given people pride in the neighborhood, and they've made other residents aware that they need to participate," Orzada said. Association members encourage others to maintain their property, she said. "If people see that the neighborhoods look shoddy, then they treat it as such," Orzada said. Besides people like Orzada who attend neighborhood meetings, Ford estimates that hundreds of people also are involved. "We're stronger in numbers. Our neighborhood has been really recognized," Ford said. "I'm sure every city official in St. Louis knows who we are."

A Hard Lesson in Politics

Just twenty-four, law student James Shrewsbury didn't realize what he was getting into when he volunteered for the re-election campaign of State Representative Ed Bushmeyer before the 1980 Democratic primary. The St. Louis Hills resident knew Bushmeyer's opponents would get ugly. He knew the 7th Ward Democratic Organization of Sorkis Webbe Sr. and Alderman Sorkis Webbe Jr. had a reputation for stealing votes by collecting absentee ballots but only mailing the ones for their candidates to election officials. The Webbes were prepared to do it again for Robert Brandhorst, their candidate for Bushmeyer's 83rd District state representative seat in the near South Side.

Bushmeyer, Shrewsbury, and other volunteers knew the only way to counter this duplicity was to arrive at the doors of people after they'd received an absentee ballot in the mail and before one of Webbe's people showed up to collect them. That way, they could receive an absentee ballot, notarize it, and mail it to election authorities. Shrewsbury apparently crossed a line when he notarized absentee ballots at the Webbe Senior Citizens Home, 1020 S. 14th Street. The home was named for former State Senator Anthony Webbe, a cousin of Sorkis Webbe Sr. The senior Webbe told two underlings—Norm Clark and Pat Gandy—to take care of Shrewsbury.

On the Friday before election day, Shrewsbury was struck in the back of the head with a blackjack as he left the Webbe Senior Citizens Home. He fell flat on his face and would have been struck again if a woman with him hadn't screamed. Shrewsbury was hospitalized for four days, suffering from a concussion, bruises, and cuts. It took him months to get back on his feet, but there were no permanent injuries. Bushmeyer narrowly won in regular voting but lost after absentee ballots were added.

What happened didn't deter Shrewsbury from being in politics, but it taught him a lesson. "I learned there are some people who will do anything to win an election," Shrewsbury said. In time, the Webbes, Gandy, Clark, and two others were indicted for mail fraud, voter fraud, obstruction of justice, and violation of civil rights for their role in the 1980 election. The civil rights violation was for Shrewsbury's beating. The senior Webbe died before the trial, but others were found guilty or pleaded guilty.

In 1983, Shrewsbury went on to be elected alderman from the 16th Ward, which includes the St. Louis Hills neighborhood. From 2001 until 2007, he was president of the St. Louis Board of Aldermen. Thus, for six years, the person holding one of the most powerful jobs in the city had a sharp memory of what a club on his head meant to silence political opposition. Shrewsbury believes instances of outright violence have declined in St. Louis politics, but this student in the school of hard knocks believes corruption remains strong among politicians.

Punch #31

Jim
Shrewsbury

Your Attentive and Aggressive Alderman

Endorsed by

St. Louis Globe-Democrat
ST. LOUIS POST-DISPATCH

Hubert H. Humphrey Young Democrats

The Shrewsbury Committee 6201 Devonshire Ave. St. Louis, Missouri 63109 353-5690
John H. Wieder, III, Treasurer

The Glamorous Board of Aldermen

To an extent, the St. Louis Board of Aldermen mirrors the U.S. Congress. It is a governing body, with each member a representative of a constituency. Aldermen approve budgets, pass laws, and okay tax breaks. These duties are the smallest aspects of their job, though. Most of the time, aldermen try to keep their constituents happy. "As an alderman, one of the things that shocked me was the volume of calls you get," said Lewis Reed, president of the Board of Aldermen. From 1999 to 2007, the Compton Heights resident was the alderman for the 6th Ward, which includes parts of the South Side's Lafayette Square, Compton Heights, and Tower Grove East neighborhoods and the western part of downtown.

Every day, he would receive twenty to fifty calls, each demanding a small amount, or sometimes a lot of help. In some cases, like a request to trim a city-owned tree between a sidewalk and the curb, a resident may get the same response by calling the Citizens Service Bureau at City Hall. In others, the only person who can deal with a situation is an alderman. While he represented the 6th Ward, Reed thought of himself as the owner of a company with just a part-time secretary and fourteen thousand customers. Others may think of the twenty-eight members of the Board of Aldermen as the mayor, king, or queen or their wards. It's natural that they would receive lots of phone calls. Within the ward, an alderman has the power to have streets paved or a zoning change approved for a new store. It goes with the job.

Most days, Reed spent his time dealing with complaints about potholes unfilled or garbage uncollected, but one call required special help. "She complained that the woman who lived next door to her was sending her bat blood in the mail," Reed said. In another case, a woman wanted a tree torn down, but when he came to the site, Reed realized the tree she wanted cut down was on private property. It also was across the street from where the caller lived. It turned out she thought the neighbors were performing certain nefarious activities in their yard and that cutting the tree down would expose them. Then there was the time he received a call from someone who had ideas about improving the Gate District, where some homes were selling for $350,000. "He said he was going to help us turn the city around," Reed said. "He said he was in housing development." So what was his idea? "He said, 'Well, trailer homes. I want to build a trailer park.'" The man promised the park would be high-class and wasn't happy when Reed said he wasn't sure it was a good idea. "He told me that's why the city would never turn around," Reed said.

Reed's experience was typical. Seventh Ward Alderwoman Phyllis Young once received a call of a personal matter. "I answered the phone, and the woman says, 'What are you going to do about my false teeth?'" said Young, a Soulard resident whose ward includes the Soulard, Benton Park, and Fox Park neighborhoods, along with the eastern part of downtown. It turned out the city health center where the woman was going to have her false teeth done was closing. Young referred her to a health center that was still open. Eighth Ward Alderman Stephen Conway, who represents parts of the Shaw, Southwest Garden, and Tower Grove East neighborhoods, once got a call from a woman griping about cats defecating on her yard. "What I didn't say to her was, 'If that's the only problem you have in life, you should consider yourself lucky,'" he said.

The Murder at Slay's Restaurant

At lunchtime at the start of the 1980s, Slay's Restaurant at 2652 Hampton Avenue was one of the favorite hangouts of local politicians. The owners were Anthony and Francis R. Slay, whose family had been influential in the city Democratic Party since the 1930s. Francis R., who operated another Slay's Restaurant in Grantwood, had been state representative and city recorder of deeds. He still was Democratic committeeman in Southwest St. Louis's 23rd Ward. Anthony was the kind of person who knew everybody who came to the restaurant, St. Louis City Comptroller Paul M. Berra told the *St. Louis Post-Dispatch*. On slow nights, Anthony would take sandwiches over to a police station nearby and talk with police officers. "He was well-liked and always had a cigar in his mouth," Berra said.

People thought the restaurant's location next to a police station protected it from crime, but it didn't help Anthony when he came to the restaurant the morning of Sunday, March 28, 1982, to unlock the door to let workers in and start work for the lunch crowd. Bobby Hines, a porter, arrived at 9:25 a.m. and found Slay bleeding heavily from the head. He was semiconscious on a chair in the dining room splattered with blood. Blood covered the floor in the kitchen and hallway. A large quantity of meat was gone from the cooler, and a company car was missing. An ambulance rushed Anthony to a hospital, where he died of extensive brain injuries at 12:20 p.m.

Early the next morning, the stolen car was found in North St. Louis. Inside was the billy club used to kill Slay. Byron Follins, who had been dismissed from his job as a porter and busboy at the restaurant, was arrested and charged with capital murder and stealing the meat. At Follins's trial, two restaurant employees said Follins had asked for their help in setting up a robbery at Slay's. Follins testified he hid in a crawl space over a walk-in freezer all day on March 27 and waited until workers left at 2 a.m. He claimed he put large amounts of meat into bags and drank beer and smoked marijuana while he waited for Slay to arrive. He wanted to use Slay's automobile to take the meat away, he said. He testified he wanted to knock out Slay, not kill him. The jury didn't believe him. They found Follins guilty of taking the meat and beating Slay to death. In April 1983, he was sentenced to fifty years in prison without parole.

SINCE 1911

Two years later, Francis R. Slay's son, Francis G. Slay, was elected alderman in the 23rd Ward. He was elected Board of Aldermen president in 1995 and mayor in 2001. As the nephew of Anthony Slay, the mayor can say with so many other city residents that he is a close relative of a murder victim.

Anthony Slay Fatally Beaten

A Decade of Fear

In the spring of 1992, a series of hideous crimes shook the South Side. For years after that, women in St. Louis Hills, Southhampton, Tower Grove South, and elsewhere didn't quite feel safe walking outside. It began on April 1, 1992, when a fifty-two-year-old woman was raped in her home near Nottingham Avenue and South Kingshighway Boulevard. On April 3, a thirty-two-year-old woman was raped in her home around Chippewa Street and January Avenue. Then on April 20, a man pressed a butter knife to the throat of a seventy-five-year-old woman in her home near Morgan Ford Road. Then he raped her. Another sexual assault followed on May 9 in a home near Hampton and Loughborough avenues.

Other rapes followed, and police stepped up their investigation of someone called the "South Side Rapist." At Francis Park, women jogged in groups. Police set up a phone line for people to call in information. Women stayed home at night, kept their windows locked, and installed new door locks. As time went on the rapist moved out of the South Side. He moved to Collinsville, Illinois, in 1994, then Arnold and St. Charles in 1995, and South St. Louis County in 1996. Police kept up their pressure against the rapist, but he stayed at large. In May 1997, about 150 people who packed the basement of St. James the Greater Catholic School in Dogtown listened as police told them to stay alert. Soon after, Police Chief Ron Henderson acknowledged police were stumped. An FBI profile suggested the rapist was clean-cut and knew the area where he struck. The rapes continued.

In October 1998 police got the break that would identify the rapist. A city detective obtained a saliva swab of Dennis N. Rabbitt, forty-two, of Cedar Hill while the policeman was investigating a report that someone was looking into windows on Alma Avenue. On November 6, the test confirmed Rabbitt indeed was the South Side Rapist. He'd been married and had a bar downtown. Those acquainted with this man, who had spent much of his life in St. Louis, said he was the last person they would have thought would have committed such crimes. Meanwhile, using the evidence, authorities in Jefferson County charged Rabbitt with the rape of an eighteen-year-old woman. Rabbitt, who had lived much of his life in South St. Louis, disappeared. Then prosecutors in St. Louis charged Rabbitt with forty criminal counts in eleven rapes.

Meanwhile, a nationwide manhunt was underway, including items in "America's Most Wanted." After three months, two Albuquerque, New Mexico, police officers arrested Rabbitt at a motel as they looked for a fifteen-year-old runaway. The girl was unharmed. Rabbitt was brought back to St. Louis. In January 2000, he pleaded guilty to forty-nine counts of sexual assault on fourteen women from 1988 to 1997. So ended a decade of terror for women on the South Side. Authorities said Rabbitt may have committed more than one hundred rapes, many in the South Side. He is serving six consecutive life sentences, which means he'll never get out of jail.

The Murdering Dentist

By day, Dr. Glennon E. Engleman fixed the teeth of patients in an office on Gravois Avenue near the Bevo Mill. By night, he had a darker side. It seemed to be a case of Dr. Jekyll and Mr. Hyde when police in 1980 got a capital murder warrant charging Engleman and another man with shooting to death Peter J. Halm of Kirkwood in 1976. Friends and people who ran businesses near his office said this was not the man they knew. But it soon became clear that his warmth and friendliness were sometime things.

It wasn't the first time police suspected Engleman of murder. The dentist was called in for questioning when James S. Bullock was gunned down with a .22 caliber pistol near the St. Louis Art Museum in 1958. At the time, Engleman's ex-wife had been married to Bullock for six months. Engleman insisted he was innocent of any wrongdoing, and police couldn't pin anything on him. Five years later, police also suspected Engleman of killing Eric L. Frey of Clayton, who worked at a dragstrip Engleman owned in Pacific. Frey died in an explosion while he tried to blow up a well in 1963. The death was ruled accidental, but authorities still speculated.

Thirteen years later came the incident that would lead to the first charges against Engleman: the fatal shooting of Peter J. Halm in 1976. It took four years for authorities to file charges against Engleman. Then Halm's wife, Carmen Miranda Halm, gave authorities the information they needed. She was a dental assistant for Engleman when he urged her to marry someone who could be murdered for insurance money. Soon after that, police moved to charge him in the car bombing that killed Sophie Marie Barrera on January 14, 1980. She had died in an explosion as she started her car outside her dental lab near the South Side National Bank. She had sued Engleman for failing to pay bills he owed the lab.

After the explosion, Ruth Engleman, one of the dentist's ex-wives, went to federal authorities. They put a wire on her and sent her back to Engleman to draw him out. In those conversations, Engleman admitted killing Barrera and said he had worked with Carmen Miranda Halm and had received ten thousand dollars from her brother after killing Halm. In his federal trial in the killing of Halm, prosecutors submitted testimony from an informant that Engleman had admitted killing Frey in 1963 for insurance purposes and dividing the proceeds with his widow.

In separate trials, Engleman was found guilty in the killings of Halm and Barrera and was given two life sentences. In prison, he pleaded guilty to the heinous murder of Arthur and Vernon Gusewelle in 1977 and their son, Ron Gusewelle, in 1979. The target in the murders of the three Edwardsville, Illinois, residents was the senior Gusewelle's half-million-dollar estate. Ron's wife, Barbara Gusewelle Boyle, was released from prison on parole in Illinois after serving half of a fifty-year sentence for murdering her husband.

Altogether, Engleman was a suspect in a dozen killings. He died at the age of seventy-one in 1999 at the Jefferson City Correctional Center. The murdering dentist was gone, but hardly forgotten.

MBER 23, 1958—32 PAGES

PRICE 5 CENTS

ENGLEMAN AGAIN REFUSES TO TESTIFY IN BULLOCK'S KILLING, BUT DENIES GUILT

A Heritage Remembered

Albert T. Jefferson had every reason to be angry at white people. As the son of ex-slaves, he surely heard story after story about injustices done by slave masters. But he spoke gratefully about the sacrifices that many whites had made for African-Americans. In his own community of Carondelet, white churches stepped in to prevent a lender from foreclosing on the mortgage of a historic African-American Church, Corinthian Baptist Church, 6326 Colorado Avenue. And he noted that white citizens of Carondelet financed Dred Scott's appeal to the Supreme Court for freedom. Those included Roswell Field, father of poet Eugene Field, and William T. Blow, father of Susan Blow, who started the first public kindergarten at the old Des Peres School in Carondelet. William Blow also donated land for the first African-American church in Carondelet. He is said to have given the land for Public School #6 (later Delaney School), the community's school for African-Americans.

Jefferson's family had come to Carondelet after the Civil War to work on a farm north of Jefferson Barracks. Jefferson was born in 1899 in the family home at 7010 Minnesota Avenue, and lived his life there as a

WESTERN NAVY YARD COMMISSION.
Rear Admiral C. H. DAVIS, Chairman.

CARONDELET CITY

From a Coast Survey Map made in
1862-63

CITY OF CARONDELET

Floating Dock.

Steamboat Ways.

Gunboat Yard.

MISSISSIPPI

bachelor. He attended the Delaney School and then Sumner High School on the city's North Side. It took him ninety minutes riding three streetcars to reach Sumner, the only city high school for African-Americans. In 1919, he took a job as a letter carrier, a job he kept all his life. An article in the old *Bugle* newspaper on December 1, 1979, recounted how Jefferson long had studied the area's black history and still was active in the Carondelet Historical Society. He died in 1989.

Jefferson lived in a community that included African-Americans long before other parts of the South Side. As early as 1850, the census counted twenty-six slaves and twenty-six African-American freedmen who worked as farmers, draymen, and servants. After the Civil War, blacks impoverished by the collapse of the plantations started moving in to find work in the community's steel mills and blast furnaces. They also worked on river packets and boats clearing the Mississippi of logs and debris. The population grew to about 450 in 1880, 600 in 1890, about 850 in 1900, and about 1,063 in 1910. The 2000 census said there were 1,847 African-Americans in Carondelet out of a total population of 9,960.

A list assembled by Jefferson showed African-Americans living in Carondelet had a variety of professions. African-Americans who lived in Carondelet included Virginia McKnight, administrator of Homer G. Phillips Hospital; Albert Burgess, a lawyer and prosecutor; John R. Steele, superintendent of buildings at Jefferson Barracks; and Hugh White Jr., a lawyer who went on to be elected to the Missouri Legislature. Lu Lu Tour (Lucille H. Schwartz), a newspaper columnist, came from Carondelet, as did Clark Terry, a musician on the staff of the Columbia Broadcasting System. Other African-Americans included firefighters, police officers, doctors, a dentist, and numerous teachers. For spiritual sustenance, most attended Corinthian Baptist Church and Quinn Chapel African Methodist Episcopal Church, 227 Bowen Street. Both remain active. Jefferson believed that whites had helped these and other institutions for African-Americans, but he still recognized and fought injustice. He picketed the old American Theater in St. Louis for segregating blacks in the second balcony and fought the barring of African-Americans from Cardinals and Browns baseball games, downtown restaurants, and other gathering places. But he was positive about his own community. "Race relations have always been good in Carondelet," he once wrote.

★ PLACES ★

The South Side's Last Mound

When Sue Maehl moved to a new house in 1963, she knew it was on top of an Indian mound, but she wasn't sure of the significance. She searched for Indian arrowheads but didn't find any. The house's location near the Mississippi River seemed more interesting. Being atop a forty-foot mound, the view was spectacular. Maehl has learned much more about that mound and its importance since she got married and moved away in 1969.

The Sugarloaf Mound is the last of about forty mounds that once dotted the city of St. Louis. The mound at 4420 Ohio Avenue is the only one that wasn't leveled to make way for development in what once was known as the Mound City. Sugarloaf was created as a part of the vast network of mounds that Mississippians created on both sides of the river from 1050 and 1400. Cahokia Mounds in Illinois have received the most attention, care, and study, but Sugarloaf Mound will have its day.

After Maehl and her two brothers moved out, their parents, Walter and Eileen Strosnider, remained. They refused to allow anyone to dig on the property, but they allowed it to be nominated to the National Register of Historic Places. The designation the mound received was important for the Strosniders, because they wanted their property preserved. They maintained that concern when they put the land up for sale in 2008. So the family was delighted when a group of concerned citizens, including U.S. Representative Russ Carnahan, contacted the Osage Nation Indian tribe in Oklahoma. The Osage Nation bought the mound in 2009. It wants to raise money to remove the houses, put fences around the property, and make it part of an educational center about the importance of the Sugarloaf Mound and other mounds. "We're thrilled. We were very happy to sell it to the Osage Indians," said Maehl, a retired schoolteacher living in California. Before her father died in June 2009, he learned the Osage Indians were interested in buying the property. He was glad they would preserve it. Her mother, who is still living, also was pleased. "She saw a lot of the articles in the paper about it. She was very impressed that where she had lived had been an important place."

The Osage Nation bought the mound because of the role they believe it played in their own history. Although their tribe is based in Pawhuska, Oklahoma, people in the Osage Nation believe their ancestors likely were among the Indians who built the Cahokia Mounds and the mounds in St. Louis. Andrea Hunter, the tribal historic preservation officer, said that early immigration stories indicate that the Osage and other tribes came down the Ohio River and then up the Mississippi to St. Louis. In addition, archaeological and anthropological evidence indicate that the social structures, rituals, games, and other practices of the Osage and the builders of the mounds were similar, she said. All this makes it likely that the Osage played an important part in the building of the mounds, she said. But Bill Iseminger, assistant manager of the Cahokia Mounds State Historic Site, offers a note of caution. It's not totally clear yet, Iseminger said. "In their oral tradition, they believe they were here some time in the past," he said. They feel a connection to the mounds in the area, he said. "There's very little archaeological evidence that either proves or disproves it." However, Hunter is convinced of the importance of preserving the Sugarloaf Mound. "Hundreds of years of our people's past were erased from the landscape in the wake of the urbanization of St. Louis," Hunter said. "There isn't anything that we can do to bring back what has happened, what was so mindlessly destroyed, but we certainly can impact what happens at Sugarloaf today."

How Caves Made Beer King

In the nineteenth century, the South Side's underground was like Swiss cheese. "Two hundred fifty years ago, St. Louis would have been a sinkhole heaven," cave explorer Joe Light said. He is president of the Meramec Valley Grotto, a chapter of the National Speleological Society that meets in the St. Louis area. Indeed, in their 1996 book, *Lost Caves of St. Louis: A History of the City's Forgotten Caves*, Charlotte Rother and Hubert E. Rother Jr. listed fifteen caves on the South Side. The reason is the mix of fairly thick limestone and dolomite bedrock formations underground in Missouri. In time, groundwater dissolves it. The vegetation, climate, and rainfall all work together to add carbonic acid to the groundwater, allowing it to dissolve minerals.

The city's nineteenth-century brewers may not have known why the caves were there, but they recognized opportunity in them. With the onset of lager beer, brewers needed a cool place to store and ferment their product, and caves fit the bill. As much as thirsty German immigrants, caves helped establish the brewing industry in St. Louis. Adam Lemp was among the biggest South Side brewers who used caves. In the early 1840s, Lemp started using a large system of caves on the road to Carondelet, now South Broadway. He first brought his beer to the caves from his brewery on Second Street, between Walnut and Elm Street, but in 1850, he built a brewery right over the cave. Another brewery, the Minnehaha, also operated briefly nearby in the same network of caves. Prohibition brought an end to Lemp's empire, but the vast buildings of his brewery still are at Cherokee Street and South Broadway.

English Cave, which is almost entirely under Benton Park, southeast of Jefferson Avenue and Arsenal Street, is another cave first used by a brewery. It was first used by Isaac McHose and Ezra English of the St. Louis Brewery in the 1840s to store their beer. Then they used it as a place to sell their product. Renamed Mammoth Cave and Park, the place offered relief from the St. Louis heat in the summer and the cold in the winter. They tried vocalists, balloon ascensions, and hiring a military band to entertain the crowds, but nothing could keep Mammoth Cave from closing.

A project to store wine there was short-lived. Using English Cave to grow mushrooms also failed, but the mushroom venture was a success at a cave at Keokuk Street and California Avenue. A *Post-Dispatch* article in 1898 reported a company was growing an average of sixty pounds of mushrooms a day in the cave.

In the 1950s, Lee Hess opened the caves formerly used by the Lemp and Minnehaha breweries to the public. Hess was a pharmaceutical manufacturer who bought land above the Minnehaha part of the cave along with the old Chatillon-DeMenil Mansion and grounds in the 1940s. He wanted to make money by having tourists visit the Lemp and Minnehaha caves. He tore down tenements and erected a museum that he intended as an entrance to the cave. As workmen made their way down, they found numerous bones. Curious, Hess sent samples to the American Museum of Natural History in New York. Geologists for the museum analyzed them and determined they were fossils of peccaries: hairy, tusked pig-like animals that died in a prehistoric flood of the Mississippi. Hess opened Cherokee Cave in 1950 and closed it when the Missouri Highway Department bought the cave, the museum building, and the historic Chatillon-DeMenil Mansion in 1961 to make way for Interstate 55. The Landmarks Association persuaded the state to move the path east, so it didn't affect the mansion. The association then got Union Electric (now AmerenUE) to put up the money to buy the historic home. As for Cherokee Cave and so many other caves under the South Side, they were sealed and filled in. They've been clogged and filled in by construction projects, rubbish, or other means, but they're evidence of the fact that an accident of nature helped make beer king on the South Side.

The Scenic River des Peres

As floodwaters from the River des Peres began to recede early on August 21, 1915, authorities made an awful discovery in a one-room cabin at 1720 January Avenue just south of Manchester Avenue. They found the bodies of David and Adeleine Bowman, their daughter Ruth, son John, and granddaughter Bessie Westmoreland. Six more bodies were found about a mile west in the suburb of Ellendale just beyond the city limits. They were killed by a normally tranquil stream that swelled to a mile wide as nine inches of rain brought by a tropical gulf storm fell in twenty-four hours on August 20–21. Altogether, 11 died and 1,025 people lost their homes. The hundreds rescued included Anna and E. G. Stange, who lived at 3600 W. Primm Street, on the west side of the river south of the present route of Interstate 55. With the river rising in their home, E. G. Stange chopped holes first in their attic and then through their roof. They were on their roof for six hours before rescue came.

The deluge—the latest and worst of five since 1897—convinced St. Louisans something had to be done to tame this little waterway that so often became a beast. Before the floodwaters had receded, Mayor Henry W. Kiel was discussing a bond issue to make the River des Peres safe. The next year, the City Plan Commission adopted a plan that included running the river underground from the city limits through Forest Park to Macklind Avenue and an open channel from Macklind to the Mississippi River. The plan also proposed running a scenic boulevard next to the river from McCausland Avenue to the Mississippi. City residents agreed on the need. In 1923, they approved an $11 million bond issue for River des Peres flood work, as part of an overall package of $87.4 million to finance improvements for the city. Workers spent the next nine years completing the River des Peres Sewerage and Drainage Works.

As many as forty-five hundred workers were kept busy doing more work on the River des Peres as part of the Depression-era Works Progress Administration. In the six miles from Pernod Avenue to the Mississippi, WPA workers installed the white stones on the side and concrete on the bottom so familiar to residents of the area today. They also created the four-mile-long River des Peres Parkway south of Lansdowne Avenue. While the work represented an improvement, for decades, people complained about the stench from the river caused by improper drainage of sanitary sewerage into the waterway.

Then in 1971, a coalition of several organizations proposed converting the six miles of the River des Peres above the Mississippi into a waterway navigable by small craft. The idea, perfect for wags who talk about the "River des Peres Yacht Club," also envisioned boating, fishing, bicycle and jogging paths, small parks, and dams and reservoirs to control water in the riverbed. The backers also suggested putting ice on the riverbed for ice skating during the winter and keeping part of the riverbed dry in the summer for fairs or art shows. Most of the plan didn't go anywhere, but today, a bike path called the River des Peres Greenway runs along the river from Lansdowne to Interstate 55. It's part of a plan by the Great Rivers Greenway to create six hundred miles of bike paths around the area. Although some may rightly call the River des Peres ugly, it's clear that work done since the 1915 flooding has made it a much safer waterway.

To Market, To Market

Behind displays of organically grown spinach, fresh cilantro, onions, potatoes, and dozens of other homegrown organic vegetables, Arlene Kruse spoke about the evils of buying processed foods from the supermarket. "Women don't care anymore. They buy in small amounts. Their tastes have changed in the fact that they don't know what good food tastes like," Kruse said. She sells the antidote in the Soulard Farmer's Market stand of Kruse Gardens of Columbia, Illinois. She started the stand in the late 1980s and has been to the market for all of her seventy-three years. Other Kruses before her had stands in Soulard. "My grandmother used to talk about coming here. So did my mother," she said above the din of the crowd.

In fact, people have been coming to the Soulard Market since 1838, when Julia Cerre Soulard donated land for use as a public market. She specified that if the property wasn't used as a public marketplace, it had to be returned to her heirs. The sign at the market claims that it began in 1779, but even the market's website acknowledges that's a myth. In 1779, St. Louis was a trading post nearly a mile away, and Soulard's market is considered the city's third public market. It is, however, the longest continually running market in Missouri, and one of the oldest in the country.

In the 1840s, a one-story building went up on the site. A second floor with a large meeting room was built in 1865. The 1896 tornado heavily damaged the building. It was repaired without the meeting room. In 1929, a new $267,000 structure replaced the old building and sheds. Its two-block-long design mirrored the Brunelleschi Foundling Hospital built around 1419 in Florence, Italy. There was room for all vendors to stay inside and a central second floor with a gym and all-purpose room. Twenty thousand people turned out for the dedication of the market on May 8, 1929.

The market stayed busy. In 1950, journalist Jim Fox wrote about it in the old *Star-Times*. "Corn from Columbia, cabbage from Commission Row and beans from Barnhart—these are but a few of the commodities for sale at bustling Soulard Market, a city institution which dates back to the early Nineteenth Century," Fox

wrote. "Today, as in earlier days, Soulard is called a farmers' market, with many of the hucksters bringing in their wares from nearby communities." "Customers come from north and south St. Louis, the East Side, the county, and, of course, the Soulard neighborhood."

Today, people are still coming, and not just for the freshest and the cheapest produce around. With nearly ninety vendors, the market offers much more than produce, including spices, meats, collectibles, breads, and even pets. Scott Androff, who works at Boeing during the week, sells his photos at the market on Saturdays. His display includes a black and white picture of someone getting into a Volkswagen behind his apartment in Soulard in 1973, color pictures of the old and new Busch Stadium, the Venice Café in Soulard, and the old Coral Court Motel. Androff started serious photography after high praise from his family. Then on New Year's Day in 1998 he made a resolution to help the market. That was the beginning of his stand. He enjoys it, but it doesn't make enough to go full-time. Another vendor, Matt Leitch, contends the secret is persistence. "Bad times get balanced out by the good times, we hope," said Leitch, of Richmond Heights, who sells incense and fragrance oil. In good times or bad, everything at the market keeps people coming back.

The Chatillon-DeMenil Mansion

The Chatillon-DeMenil Mansion has had several lives, each enough to attract visitors. Built in 1849 and expanded in 1861, the house at 3352 DeMenil Place is one of the finest surviving examples in the Midwest of the brick Southern Greek Revival homes that once filled the city, and it was once a landmark for Mississippi riverboat pilots.

The house was built by Henri Chatillon and his wife, Odile Delor Lux, both of whom had lived in Carondelet, five miles south of St. Louis. She was the granddaughter of Clement Delor de Treget, who founded Carondelet in 1771. Through his contacts in St. Louis, Chatillon met Francis Parkman, an explorer who immortalized Henri in the book *The Oregon Trail*. "His bravery was as much celebrated in the mountains as his skill in hunting; but it is characteristic of him that in a country where the rifle is the chief arbiter between man and man, he was very seldom involved in quarrels," Parkman wrote of Chatillon. A painting showing Chatillon with his first wife, an Indian squaw named Bear Robe, the daughter of the Oglala Sioux Chief Bull Bear, hangs on the mansion's wall. She died in the mid-1840s, before he married Odile Delor Lux in 1848.

The Chatillons kept the house until 1856, when they sold it to the French physician Nicholas DeMenil and Eugene Miltenberger. DeMenil's grandfather had renounced his 1,100-year-old title during the French Revolution. Nonetheless, Nicholas DeMenil still was of noble descent when he came to America on a tour. While in the New World, he fell in love with Emilie Sophie Chouteau, granddaughter of Auguste Chouteau, a founder of St. Louis. Soon they were married. In St. Louis, Nicholas owned several drug stores and was a real-estate broker. The DeMenils bought Miltenberger's share of the home in 1861 and used it as a summer retreat. DeMenil built an addition with columns and a portico. He then leased part of his land to men who wanted to start a brewery. When they couldn't pay their debts, he seized the brewery in 1867. He also built a row of homes and stores east of his home but discovered too late that the new construction ruined the view of the river. DeMenil died in 1882, and his son Alexander inherited the house.

Alexander was an attorney, literary critic, and poet. One poem defended his great-great grandmother Marie Therese Chouteau against criticism over her affair with St. Louis founder Pierre Laclede. In 1902, he took part with Mark Twain in the dedication of the steamboat *Mark Twain*. Alexander was a member of the board of the 1904 World's Fair, which explains why the mansion currently displays a large collection of fair memorabilia. Alexander died in 1928, and the mansion was maintained but not occupied.

In 1945, the family sold the home to pharmaceutical manufacturer Lee Hess. He and his wife lived in an apartment upstairs while he built a museum and made nearby caves into a tourist attraction. Cherokee Cave opened in 1950 and closed in 1961. By that time, the Missouri Highway Commission had chosen a path for the new Interstate 55 that took it through the DeMenil Mansion. Pressed by the Landmarks Association of St. Louis, the state later moved the route east but took Hess's property, including the mansion. The Landmarks Association stepped in to save the mansion. The state agreed to sell it to the association. Union Electric (now AmerenUE) put up the money for the house's purchase, while a campaign began to raise money for renovations. On May 16, 1965, the Landmarks Association transferred the building in a ceremony to the Chatillon-DeMenil House Foundation. Today's museum is a fitting memorial to the eclectic variety of people who had called the mansion home.

The Power of Politics

City Hospital was destroyed by a fire and a tornado. It had been so over-crowded that there was nowhere to put desperately ill patients. It survived wars and depressions for nearly 140 years. Yet it couldn't survive tight budgets, a decline in patients, and the political climate of the 1980s. The story of that hospital began in July 1845, when the St. Louis City Council passed an ordinance appointing a committee to choose a site and develop plans for a hospital to serve the indigent. That committee selected the present intersection of 14th Street and Lafayette Avenue. In June 1846, less than a year later, the hospital received its first patients. It was just in time for the cholera epidemic of 1849 that killed a tenth of the city's population. But less than ten years later, in May 1856, a fire razed the young city hospital. Everybody got out except an insane man who ran back in after being rescued. The next year, a new building was in place to receive the sick again, but it wasn't long before the hospital was overwhelmed. In August 1870, the hospital's supervisor gave the Board of Health a report that twenty patients were turned away in just one day because of a lack of space. Two years later, the Board of Health called the hospital a "disgrace to St. Louis" and an-nounced an effort to build a new hospital to house at least 750 patients. The existing facility was always overcrowded, and doctors often had to turn away extremely sick patients.

One wing of the new hospital had been completed by May 27, 1896, when the hospital was destroyed by a massive tornado that killed 255 people. While the city waited for a new hospital, patients were housed at the newly named Emergency Hospital 1, the Convent of the House of the Good Shepherd, in the block surrounded by 17th, 18th, Pine, and Chestnut streets. Soon the ru-ins of the old hospital became an eyesore. The *Post-Dispatch* remarked on May 28, 1897, a year and a day after the tornado, that while nearby Lafayette Park looked as pretty as ever, the hospital was even more of a wreck than the day after the storm. Meanwhile, loud critiques were heard about the condition of Emergency Hospital 1. Mayor Henry Ziegenheim promised action, but it wasn't until 1905 or 1907, depending on the sources, when a new hospital opened. Eventually, eighteen buildings in the Georgian Revival style would fill the ten-acre City Hospital site at 14th and Lafayette.

The history of City Hospital in the twentieth century was influenced by racial politics. The city opened its first hospital for African-Americans in 1919, City Hospital No. 1, at Garrison and Lawton avenues, in the old Barnes Hospital. Then in 1937, Homer G. Phillips Hospital opened at 2601 Whittier Street, named after a man who fought for its construction but was murdered before the building was completed. A system with one North Side hospital and one South Side hospital worked fine until the 1970s, when it became clear the city couldn't afford both. Those on the North Side fought suggestions about closing Homer G. Phillips. But in 1979, Mayor James Conway closed it.

This helped lead to Conway's defeat in the 1981 mayoral election. His opponent, Alderman Vincent C. Schoemehl promised he'd reopen Homer G. Phillips if he won. After he won, Schoemehl saw ballot measures needed to fulfill his promise go down in defeat. He gave up on reopening Phillips. Meanwhile, low patient counts and City Hospital's aging buildings were making it hard to keep that facility open. Black aldermen fought the idea of closing the last place in the city where the poor could be treated, but on June 22, 1985, Schoemehl announced City Hospital patients would be moved to Charter Hospital at 5535 Delmar Boulevard. Within little more than a week, one patient remained to be moved: mobster Paul Leisure. He'd been kept in the hospital's prison ward awaiting trial on murder charges. The county joined the city in creating the new St. Louis Regional Medical Center at 5535 Delmar Boulevard. It didn't last, and the indigent were left to find medical care in clogged emergency rooms.

In the years that followed, efforts to reuse the empty buildings on the City Hospital property were largely unsuccessful. By the late 1990s, windows were gone. From the streets, trees could be seen growing out of the building. Mattresses and personal items could be seen tucked into corners, signs that the homeless had moved in. But the abandoned hospital came to life again in the mid-2000s when a company led by Chris Goodson and Trace Shaughnessy developed 102 condominiums on six floors of one building facing Lafayette Avenue. More is planned for what is now called The Georgian. As with so many formerly abandoned places on the South Side, new life is coming to the old City Hospital.

The Asylum on Arsenal Street

In August 1911, the area was shocked to learn how forty-year-old Eva Jarvoubek, a patient at the City Sanitarium, was choked to death by a straitjacket she was wearing. The outcry was loud about what happened at the city's institution for the mentally ill. Dr. C. G. Chaddock, a member of the City Hospital Visiting Staff, told the State House Special Investigations Committee that the use of mechanical contrivances for quieting violent patients was wrong. Attendants too often used straitjackets and similar restraints when they should use humane care, he said. It was a brief moment of light for the institution inside a tall red brick domed building on a hill at 5400 Arsenal Street. After this incident, things went back to normal. The asylum once again became that looming building visible on the horizon throughout the South Side, where people wondered what went on inside. The asylum's history was a mix of mistreatment and sincere efforts to help mentally ill people, always limited by a lack of funding. Instances of mistreatment have declined in recent years as effective medical treatments for mental illness have become known, but increasing limits in state funding have harmed efforts to improve the lives of mentally ill people at what is now known as the St. Louis Psychiatric Rehabilitation Center.

The institution first opened as the St. Louis County Lunatic Asylum on April 23, 1869. The building went up in the country, full of fresh air thought to help mental illness, said Barbara Anderson, who was volunteer director of the hospital from 1988 to 2006. The building itself was designed to bring that air inside. But in fact, treatment of any sort was wanting. "It was basically warehousing people with mental illnesses," Anderson said. "There was no clinical criteria by which someone measured another as being psychologically disoriented," she said. Sometimes women were brought in suffering from postpartum depression and often ended up institutionalized for years. "It was a way to get rid of your wife and run around with some young girl," Anderson said. Patients also could have been alcoholics or suffering from syphilitic dementia, or just plain poor.

Treatment was cruel at worst and misguided at best. In the basement, some patients were placed in six-to-eight-foot-wide cubicles with straw on the floors. "People would defecate on the floor, and they would sweep it out every day," Anderson said. "It was cold and damp down there, and people slept on the floors." Those patients were usually African-American, or whites who were out of control. Upstairs, patients would be treated to all the amenities of the Victorian household, including reading rooms and pool rooms. These rooms also were thought to improve patients' mental health. To shock them into sanity, people were placed in vats of ice cold water. "They did the best they could, based on the incredible ignorance they had," Anderson said.

As time went on, the institution's name changed to the St. Louis City Insane Asylum and then the City Sanitarium. When the city sold it to the state for one dollar in 1948, it became the St. Louis State Hospital. In 1997, it moved to new quarters on the same property at 5300 Arsenal Street and became the St. Louis Psychiatric Rehabilitation Center. The domed building at 5400 Arsenal became an office building for the Missouri Institute of Mental Health and the State Department of Mental Health.

Through the years, as the building's name changed, one ineffective therapy replaced another. Patients danced, were given beauty treatments, and sang operettas. A newspaper ran a feature story about how straps, straitjackets, and manacles were replaced by outdoor recreation and occupational therapy, but other articles told of cramped and unsanitary conditions. Nothing really helped, though, until the discovery of medications that treated mental illness. However, here and elsewhere, their promise was limited when patients were released without enough of a structure to treat them in the community. Today, people continue to see the big building with the green dome on Arsenal Street wherever they go on the South Side. What they may not see is how budget cuts are still hurting patients.

The Golden Days of Cherokee Street

A good way to start a conversation with a septuagenarian or an octogenarian from the South Side is to ask about Cherokee Street way back when. He or she will quickly start talking about the excitement of the place, how busy it was, and how it was possible to go there and buy anything worth having. Indeed, in the 1940s and 1950s, Cherokee Street was the place to shop for people who didn't want to go downtown. There was a bit of Bedford Falls from *It's a Wonderful Life* in Cherokee Street.

The housewife who opened her *South Side Journal* on January 3, 1952, would find ads from at least a dozen Cherokee Street stores. One of them,

Fairchild's Department Store, offered quilted lined jackets for $8.88 in its January Store-Wide Sale. J.C. Penney was selling Cannon towels for sixty-seven cents in its White Goods Sale. At Morris Variety, you could buy two boxes of Kleenex for twenty-five cents.

If that housewife brought her husband to Cherokee Street that cold Friday night, they would find more than one hundred businesses in the six blocks of Cherokee Street from Jefferson Avenue west to Nebraska Avenue. They could see more than a dozen places to buy clothes, at least ten places to buy shoes, and at least seven jewelers. They would pass stores named Woolworth, S.S. Kresge, Western Auto, 905, and Walgreens. If they wished, they could buy a hat, a drink, a burger, a washing machine, a can of paint, or a sewing machine. Had they come during the day, they could have bought fresh-baked bread, brought in a suit to be cleaned, picked up a dozen roses, deposited a paycheck, gone to a doctor, or had eyes examined. But since it was Friday night, they would have to settle for watching a movie at the Cinderella or going dancing at the Casa Loma.

Within a few years, Crestwood Plaza, South County Center, and other malls opened, drawing shoppers away with them. The city's population dropped. Neighborhood shoe stores, department stores, and movie theaters disappeared. Any septuagenarian or octogenarian will say it never will be the way it was. But that's not bad. People may buy their jewelry someplace else, but there are attractions on Cherokee Street that people there sixty years ago couldn't have experienced. On a spring Saturday afternoon, people fill the outside tables of the Mexican restaurant La Vallesana at 2801 Cherokee Street. The sound of Mexican music and people speaking Spanish is heard often on the street. For those who speak English, there's the Black Bear Bakery at 2639 Cherokee Street and Foam Coffee & Beer, 3359 S. Jefferson Avenue. To the east is Antique Row, which people in the 1950s didn't have. The old times are gone, but each generation knows its own pleasures.

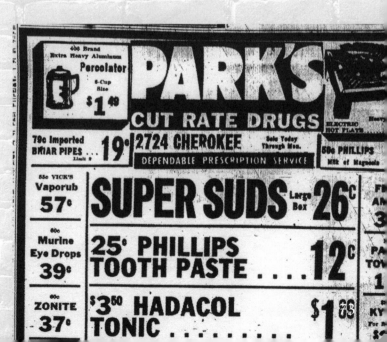

State Streets and Indian Streets

In the earliest years of St. Louis, much of the land south and west of the city was set off as common fields, communal land used for farming and grazing. By 1836, civic leaders moved toward selling this land. The boundaries of that common land were present-day Grand Boulevard on the west, Park Avenue on the north, about six blocks east of Jefferson Avenue on the east, and Delor Street on the South. The idea of organizing and naming the streets was noble—name the east-west streets for Indians or Indian tribes and the north-south avenues for states; the execution was haphazard. Today, anyone looking for order in the east-west progression of state names leading to Grand Boulevard won't find much.

As the street names were assigned, no thought was given to naming them after the original thirteen colonies, or the states of the Midwest, or putting them in alphabetical order. In order, they are, more or less, Mississippi, Wisconsin, Illinois, Missouri, and Indiana east of Jefferson. West of Jefferson are Texas, Ohio, Iowa, California, Oregon, Nebraska, Pennsylvania, Minnesota, Michigan, Virginia, Louisiana, Tennessee, and Arkansas avenues. Altogether, the city has thirty-two streets with state names, twenty-nine of which are on the South Side. After St. Louis absorbed Carondelet in 1870, many of its north-south streets assumed the names of state streets that connected from St. Louis. In 1902, five additional streets to the south were named after the states of Alabama, Colorado, and Vermont and the territories of Alaska and Idaho.

Since there is no particular order among Indian names, the order in which they are placed isn't as confusing. Many of those names have been assigned to streets west of the original commons area. Cherokee, Chippewa, Meramec, Miami, and Dakota are among the streets named for tribes. Osceola Street is named for a Seminole Indian leader who fought against Americans who tried to remove his people from their land in Florida. Potomac is named for the Potomac River. *Potomac* is an Indian word that John Smith recorded as *Potawameak*—"where goods are brought in"—in 1608.

Those names are sensible enough, but there are other east-west street names that seem like they should be Indian but are not. Itaska Street sounds like it should be Indian, but it's actually a misspelling of Lake Itasca, Minnesota. After he identified the lake as the source of the Mississippi River, Henry Rowe Schoolcraft formed the name from Latin words meaning "true source." And street names that seem to be for states actually are Indian names. The east-west Wyoming Place and Wyoming Street came from the Indian word for "land largely the big plain." The same goes for the east-west Utah Place and Utah Street, which is for the Ute or Utah Indians. Connecticut Street, which runs east to west in the Tower Grove South, Kingshighway Hills, and Tilles Park neighborhoods, adds to the confusion. It doesn't honor a state, rather an insurance company. The name of the Connecticut Insurance Company, the financier of the Tower Grove and Grand Avenue Addition of 1881, will always be remembered by those who drive along that thoroughfare.

All in a Name

Immortality is one of the privileges of building a subdivision. William Federer, a developer of the Holly Hills neighborhood near Carondelet Park, used that privilege when he named a residential street Federer Place. Developer Gus Arendes will always be remembered by residents of Arendes Drive, while developer Donald Livingston is recalled by those on Livingston Drive. To ensure their wives also were remembered forever, the three Holly Hills developers created Marwinette Avenue. It's a composite of MARie Federer, WINifred Livingston, and JeanETTE Arendes.

The St. Louis Public Library's online street index, compiled by Dr. Glen Holt and Thomas A. Pearson, is filled with such attempts to immortalize people by putting their names on street signs. Kosciusko Street on the east end of Marine Villa and Soulard is named for Polish General Thaddeus Kosciusko, who fought for the patriots in the American Revolutionary War. He became a Polish hero when he fought for independence for Poland. Tamm Avenue commemorates Jacob Tamm, a farmer and landowner. On the South Side's far west end, Jamieson Avenue honors William and James Jamieson, two brothers who were early residents of that area. Morgan Ford Road was named for a road to a ford at the River des Peres operated by a man named Morgan. Carondelet landowner Edward Haren was supposed to have his own street, but a typo in the 1882 city ordinance rendered it Haven Street. The name stuck.

Street names aren't just for people. Sulphur Avenue was developed from a road leading to a sulphur spring in David W. Graham's Sulphur Spring tract. Hydraulic Avenue in Dutchtown was named for the nearby yard of the Hydraulic Press Brick Company. Hampton Avenue is named for an urban district in Middlesex County, England. Grand is the name for a truly grand 450-foot-wide boulevard proposed in 1850 by real estate developer Hiram W. Leffingwell. In the 1860s, the St. Louis County Court set the width at a more reasonable eighty feet. From the 1800s to the early 1900s, it was Grand Avenue. Since then the city has called it Grand Boulevard. The message hasn't gotten to many who still call it Grand Avenue. South Siders don't like change.

The Broken Road

Residents of more than seven-dozen South Side streets share the same broken tale. Ten minutes after company is due at their house on Itaska Street west of Francis Park, the host receives a desperate phone call. It's the guest, in a panic. He's at Itaska Street at Ridgewood Avenue. The street just ended. What should he do? The host gives him directions and mumbles how silly it is that somebody gave the same name to an east-west street on the east side of the South Side and an east-west street on the west side of the South Side.

The question has occurred to people who live on at least ninety South Side streets. In fact, they live on at least 250 separate streets with beginnings and ends. But because they more or less were parallel, people assigned the same names to those streets, oblivious to the grief it would cause to people trying to locate addresses in the future.

In a few cases, the streets were divided by Interstates 44 and 55. The meanderings of the Oak Hill Branch of the Union Pacific Railroad through the South Side were occasionally responsible for the confusion. Sometimes a park or another major obstacle caused the road to stop. Usually, the namers could choose different names, but instead they made the decision that would cause the most confusion. So it was that there are five separate streets with the name Clifton Avenue, five named Tholozan Avenue, and five named Missouri Avenue. There are seven different streets with the name Virginia Avenue.

If an enemy takes over and we decide to confuse our invaders with our streets, we don't have to do a thing. We'll be ready.

The South Side Rolling Stop

Alderwoman Jennifer Florida has a way of aggravating constituents. It's not that she won't return phone calls or go against the wishes of residents on neighborhood issues. It's just a bad habit she picked up when she was growing up in Central Illinois. When she comes to a stop sign, she does what the sign says. "I come to an absolute stop. Sometimes people honk at me," said Florida, who represents parts of the Tower Grove South and surrounding neighborhoods. Around the South Side, it seems, most people don't have to worry about having an odd habit like Florida's. In a half-hour one Sunday afternoon, fifty westbound motorists on Fyler Avenue were spotted approaching a stop sign at Macklind Avenue. Only seven of them stopped, as in, their wheels stopped moving. Some of those apparently did so because traffic from Macklind stopped them from going forward. The others tapped their brakes with different degrees of firmness.

For what it's worth, the forty-three tappers committed a crime. The city traffic code really does require drivers to stop at a stop sign. For those who aren't sure of the meaning of "stop," the code offers a definition: "'Stop' means the complete cessation from movement." Anyone convicted of that crime must pay a fine of up to five hundred dollars and technically could spend up to ninety days in jail. Police would be ready to dispatch justice if they saw somebody committing such a crime, a police spokeswoman said. "If a motorist rolls or fails to stop, it is a violation of a city ordinance. If an officer sees this, the driver would in all likelihood be issued a ticket," spokeswoman Katie O'Sullivan said.

In the parking lot of the Shop 'n Save at 4660 Chippewa Street, people had various thoughts about the South Side stop. Will Phillips of Holly Hills acknowledged he doesn't always stop at stop signs. Whether the law should be enforced depends on the intersections, he said. Bill Wagner of the Southampton neighborhood would stop, but on one condition: "It depends whether there's a cop behind or not." Mike Pitts, a corrugated display designer living in Dutchtown, was alarmed when he learned how few people halt their vehicles at stop signs. "That's scary," he said. "I come to a complete stop. I aggravate a lot of people, but I do it anyway."

If just about everybody on the South Side goes through stop signs, there's good reason. There's about eighteen thousand stop signs in the city, compared with about six hundred traffic signals, Street Commissioner Todd Waelterman said. When people encounter three or four stop signs in ten blocks, it's easy to nudge the brake rather than press down hard, especially when the cops don't care. And yet people keep asking for more. "Certainly, I think we oftentimes misuse stop signs," Waelterman said. People try to use them to slow motorists down, Waelterman said. Neighbors keep pressuring for more signs. When people ask for a sign, the street department makes a study to see if it's needed. But regardless of what that recommendation might be, an alderman is still free to put forth a bill requiring another sign. "The neighborhood pressure is so great that it winds up becoming an ordinance and we wind up putting up a sign," Waelterman said.

Florida sees the pressure in her own ward. "People think that's the quick fix," she said. "You put up a stop sign, and people roll through it." She once sought to have police ticket all violators. "It's enforcement that really changes behavior in neighborhoods," she said. But the request didn't go anywhere. Instead, the stoppers keep on rolling, and rolling, and rolling.

The Street that Ends with a Stairway

On the South Side, some streets stop at circular concrete barriers set side by side. Some end at gates, some at Interstates 44 and 55, and some at railroad tracks. Others end at fences or at a river, but one street in the Gravois Park neighborhood halts in a completely different way: at a stairway. Motorists driving south on Oregon Avenue from Potomac Street toward Miami Street find that it suddenly stops at a stairway marked by a high wrought-iron fence. The fence is on the top of a concrete retaining wall that drops down eight feet. A car thief who is speeding away from police at 120 miles an hour might not want to choose southbound Oregon at Potomac for his escape path. Otherwise, if he was able to plow through the fence, he would find himself airborne in the best tradition of movie chase scenes.

The city's Board of Public Service apparently put up the wall at the behest of Oregon Avenue property owners who didn't like the way the street sloped. In the early 1920s, it filled with two- and four-family flats. In 1928, the Board of Aldermen passed an ordinance requiring property owners on the block to pay for a project to flatten out the street and make it end at a fence on top of an eight-foot retaining wall. Pedestrians could use the steps to walk from the lower part of Oregon to the upper part. More than eighty years after the project, Mike Seemiller of the Board of Public Service remarked that he'd never seen anything like this before. "This is a real unusual case," said Seemiller, whose agency is in charge of street construction.

The oddity benefits people like Sam Brown. He's a carpenter who lives in a four-family flat just north of the fence. "There's no through traffic. I like that part of it," Brown said. Pedestrians once could walk on a sidewalk to an opening in the fence and then go down a stairway, but that way through has been closed, to the consternation of some walkers. "I saw a man this morning walking. I saw him walk down to that fence and just look," said Jim Roos, who manages most of the four-family flats that line the street. It's not often that drivers or walkers come into the street and discover it stops, Roos said. By now, most people know that the street dead-ends, he said, but the way it dead-ends is like nowhere else.

The South Side's Hidden Railroad

Just before 9:30 on a Wednesday morning in June, an engine, four cars carrying freight, and a caboose crossed McRee Avenue east of Kingshighway Boulevard. Soon, a track took them under Interstate 44 as the train started a seven-mile winding trip through the South Side. The St. Louis, Oak Hill, and Carondelet Railway built the line in 1887. For more than 120 years, trains have made that trip, which snakes west, just west of Tower Grove Park, and southeast to the edge of Carondelet Park before heading south to the city line. Today, an average of four trains a day use the tracks, which are part of Union Pacific Railroad's DeSoto Subdivision from McRee Avenue to Poplar Bluff. People generally see the trains when they cross streets, but mostly the trains and the tracks they use are hidden by buildings, trees, brush, and by their location below street level. When they see the trains crossing a variety of different streets, motorists may think there's several lines on the South Side. But outside of the track that runs along the river, this is the only rail line south of Interstate 44 in the city.

After emerging from under Interstate 44 from McRee, the trains travel northwest of Vandeventer Avenue until they go underneath the Kingshighway viaduct. They pass Bischoff Avenue before traveling under Southwest and Columbia avenues on the east side of Marconi Avenue. Customers of Favazza's Restaurant on the Hill at Southwest and Marconi may not realize it, but their parking lot is just a few feet from train tracks. They can't see them because the tracks are below grade and because trees, brush, and a fence hide them, but if they come close to the trees and look through the brush, they will see the tracks, along with graffiti on the bridge on Southwest Avenue. More graffiti is evident to a person standing on the far side of the Columbia Avenue bridge over the rail line. It covers a healthy portion of the side of a building owned by Ralston Purina at 5100 Columbia Avenue.

The train tracks continue below street level, between the industrial buildings on Hereford Street to the east and a mix of industries and old houses on Brannon Avenue to the west. Shoppers at the Schnucks on Arsenal Street may not know that train tracks are just west of the parking lot unless they use the crosswalk of the bridge over the tracks. The tracks continue out of sight until they come in view on the trestle above Kingshighway just south of Home Depot. They're visible again from a bridge over the tracks on Morgan Ford Road near Fairview Avenue. The tracks continue on bridges over Chippewa Street and Gravois Avenue before mostly staying behind industrial buildings around Gustine, Ulena, and Dewey avenues. Things may look inviting a hundred feet away, on the other side of the trees and overgrowth, but there is plenty of dirt, trash, and graffiti along the rail line.

From the north, the rail line goes under the bridge leading from Grand Boulevard into Carondelet Park. It passes under another bridge leading from the west part of the park to the Carondelet Park Recplex. Those who drop off their papers or aluminum cans in the park's recycling center can see a long open section of the tracks. South of the spot, the tracks go under Loughborough Avenue and by the Loughborough Commons Shopping Center. From there, they go under Interstate 55, between Alabama and Alaska avenues and out of the city. Their route is on city maps, but most people don't notice. Though the rails are in the South Side, for most they're in another world.

South Side National Bank

Unlike many major street corners, there is no Walgreens at Gravois Avenue and Grand Boulevard. That's good, because if there was one a key link to the area's past would be gone. In the late 1990s, neighborhood groups stopped the demolition of the South Side National Bank at the southwest corner of Grand and Gravois and its replacement by a smaller bank building and a Walgreens. The grand ten-story Art Deco building the preservationists saved was seen as a sign the good times would go on forever when it opened just before the start of the Depression. A booklet put out when it opened on January 2, 1929, called it "The Dawn of a New Day for Grand and Gravois."

Like so much on the South Side, Anheuser-Busch had a hand in the bank. Beer baron Adolphus Busch founded the South Side Bank at the beginning of the 1890s. The Busches stayed involved in the bank at Broadway and Pestalozzi Street and its successor, the South Side Trust Co. Busches were on the bank board in 1927 when it voted to buy land on the southwest corner of Grand and Gravois for a new building. The next year, the bank merged with Farmers and Merchants Trust, which was on the southeast corner of Grand and Gravois.

With the strength of two banks, the owners had reason for optimism when they opened the new building in 1929. "The Dawn of a New Day" spoke of how the bank was on the second floor, accessible by a grand staircase and an elevator "to give you and the other citizens of South St. Louis first-class protection." Apparently, they thought that would discourage bank robbers. But protection from bandits didn't protect the bank from closing and reorganizing during the Depression. Nonetheless, a bank stayed at the corner through changes in the area and the attempt to tear it down.

In 2001, after neighborhood groups saved the building, Allegiant Bancorp Inc. gave the building to the Grand Oak Hill Community Corp., a neighborhood group for the area. Grand Oak Hill later gave it to The Lawrence Group, a local architectural firm. The Lawrence Group rehabbed the building for thirteen condominiums on seven top floors and improved three bottom floors for commercial use, but the economic downturn slowed efforts to occupy the whole building.

Residents of the building—now called the South Side Tower—can ease their worries about that downturn or anything else by going to its rooftop. There, they have a hawk's eye view of the South Side, downtown, and the building Walgreens put up when it couldn't tear down the South Side National Bank.

A Historic House Holds the Cards

An oversized photograph of nearly sixty members of the Carondelet Park Pinochle Club in 1986 hangs on a wall in an old white two-story frame house on the east side of Carondelet Park. Across from the picture on a Tuesday morning early in 2010, four members of the club played the game on a worn particleboard table. None were younger than seventy-eight. The twenty-five or so men on the club's roster included some who were younger, but not by much.

The club is much smaller than it once was, but those who still come to play cards on weekdays love the game. "I always did like to play pinochle since I was a kid," said Cliff Portelli, a retired letter carrier who comes by about three or four days a week. Charles Puricelli, a retired chemical operator, started coming about 1994. "It's just like going fishing. You want to catch that great big fish," Puricelli said. "It's a social club. Everybody's friendly. It keeps your mind busy so you don't get that Alzheimers." Gene Paszkiewicz has been coming two or more times a week for about a dozen years. The retired job site supervisor for a construction company likes the camaraderie. "I wish there was more people wanting to play the game," he said.

Like members of the club, the house that they play in is showing signs of age. Wallpaper is faded, and tile floors are dirty and in need of replacement. Some walls have holes in them. Known as the Lyle House, it is one of the more recognizable houses on the South Side. The builder was Alexander Lacy Lyle, a carpenter and successful businessman who was born in 1804 near Lexington, Virginia, and died in the home in 1874.

CARONDELET PARK PINOCHLE CLUB

Carondelet Park was established two years after Lyle's death, and for decades the house served as the home of the park superintendent.

The pinochle club leases the building from the city for a nominal fee and pays for items like paper products, the phone bill, and insurance from a membership fee. Aldermen Matt Villa, D-11th Ward, and Fred Wessels, D-13th Ward, who share Carondelet Park, also provide money from funds allocated for their wards. Wessels, whose father long played pinochle at the club, noted the parking lot by the house is filled as early as 7 a.m. with cars of men anxious to play. Work is planned on the outside in 2011. While some work also is needed inside, "It's functional for the needs of the card players," Wessels said.

"We're satisfied with the place. We just come here to play pinochle," former Club President Joe Holway said. Five or six times a year, the group holds luncheons from deer chili provided by Paszkiewicz. The Holly Hills Improvement Association occasionally holds meetings at the Lyle House, but the club is left mostly on its own to operate the building. For now, the question is how long men will keep taking tricks.

Holding True in Tower Grove

In a shady spot in Tower Grove Park on a Sunday afternoon, a mother places a tablecloth on a picnic table. In a language other than English, she calls her husband and children to sit down. Lunch is about to begin. Members of other families walking on paths nearby are also talking in a language other than English, but not the language of the family preparing for a picnic lunch. It's a story that could have been told about the park in 1900 or 2010. In the earlier period, the non-English languages of park users could have been German, Polish, or Italian. Today, it might be Vietnamese, Bosnian, or Spanish.

The story told by Tower Grove Park Director John Karel is one example of what he sees as an enormous consistency in what has gone on at the park for more than 140 years. The vision Missouri Botanical Garden founder Henry Shaw had when he gave St. Louis land for the park in 1868 is to a large degree a reality today. Cars long ago replaced horse buggies as the way to traverse the park, but the park that visitors see today is much the same as the one Mark Twain praised following a visit during an 1882 tour of towns and cities along the Mississippi River. In *Life on the Mississippi*, Twain wrote that Tower Grove Park, Forest Park, and the Missouri

Botanical Garden were notable among the fine parks of St. Louis. The map he would have used to travel the park is the same as visitors now use.

Many of the structures Twain saw in 1882 still serve the same purpose. Stable buildings are still stable buildings. Mock ruins assembled from what was left after a fire destroyed the first Lindell Hotel in 1867 are still there. So are the water lilies. Statues Shaw donated of Shakespeare, Mozart, and others are as he left them. Music is still heard weekly in the summer, but at a different time. In the nineteenth century, it was from 4 p.m. to 6 p.m. on Sundays, when people of all classes could come. Today, the Compton

Heights Concert Band plays at 7:30 p.m. on Mondays. And, if Twain were to return today, he would find the four stone main entrances the same as the last time he was here.

Karel acknowledges there are differences between the park today and the one of the late nineteenth century. Nonetheless, the similarities are strong enough to make Tower Grove almost unprecedented among American parks, Karel contends. As before, thousands of trees cover the 289-acre park surrounded by Grand Boulevard, Arsenal Street, Kingshighway Boulevard, and Magnolia Avenue. Karel speculates that about 120 of the park's trees are original. Many other trees among the 6,500 or so also are old but probably were planted after Shaw died in 1889, Karel said. And there are new uses, including the farmer's market that now operates in the park in the spring, summer, and fall.

Though the park long was a treasure, many worried that it would be lost. That's what people thought when Karel became director in 1987. "It didn't seem to be a sure thing that we were going to survive," said Karel, who directed Missouri's state park system from 1979 to 1985. But along with other South Siders, he was determined to stop the decline. "We weren't going to go down without a fight," Karel said, but there were reasons for discouragement. The Piper Palm House, built to house palms in 1878, was used as a garage. The roof was leaking, and mortar was crumbling from between rows of bricks, but after restoration, the building became an elegant place for Sunday brunches and receptions. Its acoustics make it a favorite place to hear members of the St. Louis Symphony Orchestra perform works by Beethoven and Mozart. The success of the Piper Palm House was contagious throughout the park. Henry Shaw established a board to govern the park, while the city was charged to maintain the land. But private donors raised the millions of dollars necessary to complete the restoration. Today, the park is a place of wonder for those who come for a visit, be they from across the street, West County, or China. Whatever they say, and whatever the visitors' language, their words would please Shaw if he were to hear them today.

A Dome Saved a Garden

From 1960 on, people were excited about Shaw's Garden in a way they hadn't been in years. Shaw's Garden was what people half a century ago called the Missouri Botanical Garden. Whatever people called it, the buzz was about a new attraction that opened late in 1960 to replace the outdated Palm House: the Climatron. One geodesic dome modeled after the designs of R. Buckminster Fuller, the upside-down plexiglass-enclosed bowl showed all that was possible in a greenhouse. It was 70 feet high, 175 feet in diameter, and covered three-quarters of an acre. In a tropical environment, it contained banana plants, coffee plants, palms, and a whole array of other tropical and semi-tropical plants owned by the garden.

After it opened in October 1960, the papers gushed about this building that offered different climates, depending where a person was in the dome. "The gleaming transparent dome of aluminum and plexiglass is the climax of a long chain of engineering triumphs, some laboriously arrived at and inconceivable without the aid of electronic computers, others the result of brilliant improvisations," the *Post-Dispatch* said in an article titled, "The Climatron as Architecture." In an article written in the coldest days of January 1961, the *Globe-Democrat* spoke of the St. Louisan imagining he was in a warmer place. "In his dreams of escape to Caribbean islands or remote spots south in the sun, he may overlook a place considerably closer—the Climatron in Missouri Botanical (Shaw's) Garden."

THE ☆CLIMATRON☆

The superlatives attached to the Climatron were great, but the biggest one was how it turned around a slide in attendance at the Garden that started with the Depression. So few people paid to get in that the Garden couldn't afford to change exhibits. Buildings were in poor shape. The future looked grim. But then came the Climatron, along with thousands of people willing to pay the fifty-cent admission fee at the new attraction. Attendance, which had been as low as 156,297 in 1955, climbed from 279,800 in 1959 to 423,302 in 1960. It kept increasing from there. Today, more than 970,000 people come to the Garden each year. It's possible Shaw's Garden wouldn't have developed into the marvel for visitors and researchers that it is today if the Climatron hadn't been built.

Naked Truth

The intent was innocent enough: Put up money to find somebody to make a monument to the way three journalists showed the German-American spirit in St. Louis. So why were people yelling? Well, the monument was of a woman, and she wasn't wearing clothes, and this was 1913. So it was that 250 people sent letters condemning the design of German sculptor Wilhelm Wandschneider for a memorial to honor the journalists Carl Schurz, Emil Preetorius, and Carl Daenzer. Wandschneider was on his way from Germany to accept the commission, and the committee that chose the design was looking for a way out.

All three of the journalists had been editors of the local German newspaper the *Westliche Post*. Schurz had been a Civil War general, a senator from Missouri, and Secretary of the Interior under President Rutherford Hayes. A group formed to honor them, and Adolphus Busch of Anheuser-Busch put up $20,000 for a memorial—nearly $430,000 in 2009 dollars. Others added more. The competition began. When it was over, a committee accepted Wandschneider's design of a seated nude woman holding torches in each of her outstretched arms. He called it "The Naked Truth."

Then the protests began. Busch said the design was too startling to accept. The $30,000 contract and $1,000 bonus were withdrawn. It was too much for Dr. Frederick Kolbenheyer, who had headed a committee that had selected Wandschneider's design out of seven considered. "Gentlemen," he said to the directors of the Schurz-Preetorius-Daenzer Memorial Association, "You are a lot of damned fools. I resign." The nude woman's figure typified the naked truth the three great German-American editors fought for, he said. "The torches which the figure holds in each hand are for the enlightening of Germany and America." An editorial in the *St. Louis Post-Dispatch* said the Naked Truth was a frequent troublemaker.

Meanwhile, Wandschneider sailed for the United States with his wife to accept his prize. When he arrived in New York, he threatened to sue or set off an international incident if he didn't get it. He refused an offer to compromise by draping the lady with lingerie. When he showed up in St. Louis on

May 29, the statue was big news. The committee that made the selection wasn't sure what to do. After a hot May, some said Wandschneider had clad the woman for St. Louis summers. The *St. Louis Globe-Democrat* remarked that the Naked Truth may be a fine monument for some newspapers, but reputable newspapers don't print every truth they hear, the paper said, because they learned it in confidence or it may hurt innocent people.

Then Busch announced he'd taken a good look at a model of the statue. It was fine, he said, adding that he'd drawn his first conclusions after looking at sketches. That was enough for the board of the association that commissioned the monument. It voted 12–2 in favor of Wandschneider's design. The statue was dedicated for all to see on May 27, 1914, in Compton Hill Reservoir Park on South Grand Boulevard near the present site of Interstate 44.

Other pitfalls were ahead for the statue. After the United States entered World War I, some suggested the statue be melted down for cannonballs meant for Germans. Fortunately, the idea remained only a suggestion. In the 1960s, it was moved out of the path of the new Interstate 44. In recent years it started looking seedy. Graffiti artists dabbed paint on her toenails, fingernails, and lips. It fell to neighborhood groups to raise

money to restore the lady. Today, the statue sits peacefully in Compton Hill Reservoir Park as a monument to a time when naked truth was an embarrassment.

The Frog of Chippewa Street

Even partially covered by various shades of blue and purple paint, the Frog of Chippewa Street carries a kind of dignity. Crouched in the middle of what once was a vacant lot at Chippewa Street and Oregon Avenue, the frog stands four feet high and is five and a half feet long and four feet wide. The statue had no ordinary beginning. It is one of about forty concrete cast frogs made by Bob Cassilly, who created Turtle Park near Forest Park and founded the City Museum downtown. Once people bought the frogs, they wound up in all kinds of places. One of those places was a quarter-acre vacant lot that once was the location of a 7-Eleven convenience store. Mark Rice, who lives a few blocks away, got a grant to buy the frog and place it on the lot. It was meant to be a sign that the area was hopping back. But at times things seemed more like the place was croaking.

Before the frog came, the appearance of the place wasn't particularly inviting. The 7-Eleven was torn down, but the empty lot was filled with junk cars and broken glass. The frog brought hope and plenty of promises from people to help Rice keep it up. Nobody followed through. Rice maintained the property for a while before he gave up. Almus "Slim" Cox, a business and community leader and the longtime owner of Slim and Zella Mae Cox Furniture next to the lot, said he and his wife had tried to maintain the park, but they grew too old and couldn't continue.

THE FROG -of- CHIPPEWA ST.

So it was that for some years people cut the grass regularly and kept up the plants. In other years, it became overgrown until nobody could see the frog. Paint once applied by a group of volunteers started chipping off, leaving strange splotches. More recently, the Chippewa-Broadway Business Association offered a hand to bring out the best in what became known as the Frog Garden.

With their help, groups such as workers from a nearby branch of Regions Bank and the group Faith Beyond Walls installed planter boxes, put in mulch and wood chips, and planted flowers, including daffodil bulbs donated by the Missouri Botanical Garden. The work of the volunteers is made more difficult by the fact that nobody really owns the park. The land is registered to something called the Chippewa-Broadway Jefferson Association, but that group no longer exists. Only time will tell how long the work of the volunteers at the Frog Park will continue. As of the summer of 2010, the volunteers have tended the frog's garden. But whatever happens in the future, nothing can take away the dignity of the Frog of Chippewa Street.

More Than Good, an Institution

On a parking lot on Chippewa Street a plastic spoon rested amidst a runny brownish-white glob. A minute before, it was a medium Ted Drewes hot fudge concrete with a spoon in the middle, but then the holder of that treasured treat turned it over to test the claim that if you held a concrete upside-down, it will stay in place, along with the spoon. It stayed in the cup for only a moment before plopping to the ground. Crestfallen, but still craving what only Ted Drewes can offer, the man who turned the concrete over eventually made his way back to a window and bought another one.

The failed experiment took place early on a dreary Saturday evening in May amidst a more modest crowd compared with the hot August weekend evening throngs that spill out onto Chippewa, but the group of customers still was big enough that the windows had constant lines. Among those who had come was a woman with bright pink hair, a wedding party, a couple and their four children on vacation from Minnesota, and people who had returned from afar to taste this South Side delight.

Walt and Kim Wiseman stop by every time they make the eighty-mile trip to St. Louis. Kim's grandmother lives near the Bevo Mill, so they come in about once a month. "Best place to eat ice cream," said Walt, a carpenter, eating his Dutchman. Kim usually buys the Dutchman, but this time she tried something new, the Christy. Their son Danny feasted on a large Dutchman concrete. Pete and Pat Lecko and their twenty-year-old son David only had to travel from South St. Louis County to come to Ted Drewes. They come about twice a month. Pat grew up not far from the Ted Drewes at 4224 S. Grand Boulevard and always went there. "I think it's great ice cream," Pat said. "I've been to other custard places. I don't like them as much as here." David, who attends Missouri University of Science and Technology at Rolla, pledges his eternal devotion. "I'll be coming here my entire life. The ice cream's so good."

It's pretty well known around St. Louis how the Ted Drewes stores came about. In 1929, Ted Sr. opened his first store in Florida. He opened another one on Natural Bridge Road in 1930 and then the South Grand outlet in 1931. Ten years later, the Chippewa store opened. The Natural Bridge location closed in the late 1950s, leaving just the two on the South Side. Ted Jr., who's now in charge, has often said he's turned down numerous offers to franchise his operation because it could lead to a mediocre product. Instead, he has worked on building up a loyalty that crosses generations. People love this place and what comes out of it, even if the concretes don't stay in the cup. The loyalty extends so far that a trip to Ted's is another ritual of life in St. Louis, for residents and visitors alike. Patrons believe the Ted Drewes slogan, "It really is good, guys, and gals."

It's terrific, but it's still just fancy ice cream. Other places sell frozen treats that might beat a Ted Drewes concrete in a blind taste test, but people don't stand in line in August when the mercury's passed one hundred to buy one of those other items. Hungry customers don't routinely stop at other establishments before the prom or after a meal at Charlie Gitto's on the Hill. Something else happened to elevate Ted Drewes to the short list of must-see places for tourists to go when they're in St. Louis. Things came together. It helped that the main store is on historic Route 66 close to everything. It's wholesome and clean, which makes it a great place to bring the kids and for teenagers to hang out. When those kids and teenagers grow up, they'll bring their kids and teenagers to Ted Drewes. Then there's the ritual people go through to buy and consume something at Ted Drewes. Get into a line spilling out onto Chippewa, wait, order, pay, take the treat, stand around with others, and roll that cold goodness around in your mouth. It's an odd ritual, but pleasant, the kind of experience that makes for tradition. Let people all over St. Louis experience it, along with tourists and former St. Louisans back for a visit, and the tradition becomes an institution.

Saving the Feasting Fox

Martin and Susan Luepker owned a healthy heating and air conditioning business that Martin's grandfather started in 1896. The couple knew nothing about the restaurant business. So why would they want to acquire a broken-down old building, renovate it, and run a European-style restaurant there? All good questions. The answer boils down to the fact that they didn't want the Dutchtown neighborhood to lose a historic building that was part of the effort of Anheuser-Busch to stave off Prohibition. Today, their Al Smith's Feasting Fox Restaurant is a popular place full of antiques and brewery collectibles known for its American and German dishes.

In 1914, August Busch Sr. opened the Gretchen Inn at South Grand Boulevard and Meramec Street. It was the second of three close-by restaurants that the Busches opened in the same decade. The Stork Inn at Virginia and Taft avenues was built in 1910, and the Bevo Mill at Morgan Ford Road and Gravois Avenue in 1917. The Gretchen Inn was a popular place along busy Grand Boulevard, in part because of a racetrack on the southwest corner of Meramec and Grand called Priester's Park.

The coming of Prohibition in 1920 brought more changes to the building than the removal of alcohol from the menu. It became a store where legal products made by Budweiser, such as vitamins, ice cream, soda, and spices, were sold. After the repeal of Prohibition in 1933, antitrust laws wouldn't allow a brewery to operate a place where drinks were sold. So the brewery leased it to Al Smith, who operated it until 1961. Then Fred and Evelyn Krumm, who had managed the restaurant since 1945, took over. After it closed in 1986, the building started falling apart. In 1993, Anheuser-Busch took steps to sell it to a fast-food restaurant.

Neighbors wouldn't have it and started noisy and well-publicized protests. The brewery backed down and said it would entertain other proposals. Then the Luepkers reluctantly entered the picture and agreed to take on the project. "We thought more or less if we didn't do it there's nobody else who would," Martin said. So the couple plowed ahead to renovate a building that was structurally solid but otherwise a mess. The windows were boarded up, parts of the roof were missing, and the ceiling had collapsed over the kitchen. All of the original woodwork was gone. As they did their renovations, they looked for furniture from other old restaurants: Top of the 230 in Clayton, the Missouri Athletic Club, the old Dohack's Restaurant on Lemay Ferry Road, and Nantucket Cove. "The building wanted to live. Whatever we needed came," Martin said. Publicity over the opening in 1994 brought more business than the Luepkers could handle. In 1997, the couple opened the Gretchen Inn for banquets in an adjacent building. It's been a major part of the business. Today, the restaurant is filled with a wide mix of memorabilia. One framed 1896 picture shows a print of Union Station by the Anheuser-Busch Brewing Association. Another shows Custer's Last Stand. One old sign reads "Best Since 1867 Leinenkugels Chippewa's Pride."

Customers seem pleased with the restaurant's fare. "I love the Feasting Fox. I love coming in here because of the eclectic atmosphere," said Vicki Gallant, who has lived in the neighborhood for ten years. "We've been coming here for years, and we know Martin and Sue, the owners," said Shannon Olson, a Florissant resident who was eating lunch with her family. The next step is uncertain for the Luepkers. "Sooner or later, we're going to be too old. We haven't anyone in our family that's interested," Martin said. But Susan has confidence in its future. "Just like in the beginning, the building wanted to be saved and it will be again," she said.

The Bevo Mill

The oft-told tale on the South Side is that Anheuser-Busch President August Busch Sr. built the Bevo Mill at Morgan Ford Road and Gravois Avenue as a place to rest halfway between the Anheuser-Busch brewery and Grant's Farm, but the big reason was to fight the Prohibitionist idea that alcohol was evil and that places serving alcohol were not for polite people. Busch wanted to show that people could enjoy light wine, a beer, or near-beer with good food and the atmosphere of a German family garden.

In June 1917, the restaurant opened in a $200,000 structure with a tower supporting a Dutch windmill. It seated seven hundred inside and out. Busch wanted to give the place an Old World feel. And one way was with a new near beer called Bevo. Bevo, beer, and light wine were the only adult beverages available.

The Bevo Mill became a popular attraction, but it wasn't without its detractors. In their book, *Under the Influence: The Unauthorized Story of the Anheuser-Busch Dynasty*, Peter Hernon and Terry Ganey wrote that in spite of what Busch said, patrons of German saloons preferred hard liquor over the less intoxicating variety. "More serious, the idea ran afoul of wartime hysteria," they wrote. "There were cries that the mill, with its slowly revolving blades and Teutonic menu featuring such heavy delicacies as bratwurst glockein, was an insideous attempt to force German ways upon patriotic St. Louis."

But the Bevo Mill survived those attacks as it survived Prohibition. It stayed on as a South Side landmark and a favorite place to order sauerbraten. It gave its name to the surrounding neighborhood. In 2009, it survived the sudden closing of its doors that caused many to lose deposits they had placed on wedding receptions. Today, under new owners, it is again a destination for Sunday brunch and a place for wedding receptions. It remains one of the brewery's biggest gifts to the South Side.

The Casa Loma

If a big band was big, it made it to the Casa Loma ballroom. Glenn Miller was there. So were Tommy Dorsey, Guy Lombardo, Duke Ellington, Louis Armstrong, and Frank Sinatra. Bill Haley and the Comets rocked around the clock at the ballroom at 3354 Iowa Avenue. For decades, men in suits and women in fancy dresses packed the dance floor of the place around the corner from the Cherokee Street shopping district. Today, they're still coming. Pat Brannon, who owns the ballroom, brings in eighteen- to twenty-four-piece big band orchestras on Fridays, old-time rock 'n' roll or swing on Saturdays, and Hispanic dances with out-of-town bands on Sundays.

Brannon was sales manager for a fence company when he bought the ballroom in 1990. "I just happened to come in and saw it was for sale," Brannon said. "I'd been an Imperial swing dancer for years and had always been on the outside of the bar and figured it wouldn't be that hard to be on the inside of the bar," he said. "They haven't kicked me out yet." Crowds vary. "You can have three hundred on a Saturday night, or you can have six hundred," Brannon said. He maintains diverse acts. For lovers of the big bands, he's had Larry O'Brien and the Glenn Miller Orchestra and Guy Lombardo's Royal Canadians with Al Pierson. For those who crave a different sound, he's had Sh-Boom, Butch Wax and the Hollywoods, and the Smash Band.

The ballroom itself looks pretty much like pictures of the original Casa Loma. Balcony seating is available on three sides, and the raised stage is on the fourth. On either side of the stage, banners advertising Corona Extra hang down. On one side of the stage is a black-and-white drawing of a 1930s-era man in a tux with a woman in formal dress. Black tables and chairs surround the hardwood dance floor. Near the entrance, a bulletin board displays pictures of such stars and groups as Bob Kuban, Gateway City Big Band, and Hudson and the Hoo Doo Cats. A stairway leads to the entrance.

On the Saturday afternoon of Memorial Day weekend in 2010, a different kind of entertainment was planned. Steve Vollenweider, a college student studying architecture, was preparing for a benefit for the American Diabetes Association that night. The Hill resident organized live music tributes to Nina Simone, Johnny Cash, Elvis Presley, and Michael Jackson. He rented the place hoping to bring in lots of cash for his cause. He had reason for choosing the Casa Loma. "Casa Loma is very historic, and it's something that I believe we should support in this city," he said.

The venue's history began when a building with a ballroom was put up on that site in 1927. In his book *St. Louis Casa Loma Ballroom*, David A. Lossos noted there were five different attempts to open a ballroom there, beginning with one called Cinderella Hall. All failed. Art Kawall and H. J. "Nap" Burian tried again in 1935. They took the name Casa Loma from the popular Glen Gray's Casa Loma Band. Success followed, and the Casa Loma brought in groups that included the Count Basie Orchestra and Skitch Henderson, who later played on *The Tonight Show*. It seemed that nothing could go wrong, but something did. On the bitterly cold evening of January 19, 1940, a fire destroyed the building. Marvin "Bud" Miller was sixteen when he witnessed the fire. He recalled his impressions in a March 27, 1994, article about the blaze in the *South Side Journal*. "It was amazing to watch. Of course, this was a landmark place . . . to see all of this destruction, and to see all these men performing in that bitter cold, it was just incredible." The work of the firefighters that night was one of the reasons he made firefighting a career.

The damage was total, but the hunger for the big band sound was great. On November 15, 1940, Herbie Kay and His Orchestra performed on reopening night of the rebuilt Casa Loma. In the war years that followed, the area needed the good times the dance hall provided. At its height, as many as three thousand came out. The place was open six nights a week. But time changed. Burian died in 1958. By the 1960s, the Casa Loma was open three nights a week. The Kawall family sold it in 1967. Music was offered both for a younger and an older crowd. Although attendance was down to four to five hundred a night, it was still profitable. It kept being profitable. Some would say that a place started for the musical tastes of the 1930s wouldn't be around in the twenty-first century, but ballroom music remains popular, which keeps the Casa Loma humming.

The Pelican's Sad End

For years, people remembered the restaurant at 2256 S. Grand Boulevard for the twenty-five-foot blue pelican sign. The establishment had a variety of owners and names, but its longest tenure went by the name Pelican's, named after its owner James Pelican, who began operations in the 1930s.

As early as 1875, people were eating and drinking at that location. Three years later, one C. Becker was given a building permit to build an addition to the "existing saloon and dwelling." A 1979 *Globe-Democrat* story said that the Griesedieck family of brewers, which later bought Falstaff Brewing Co., was the owner during this period. In 1895, the family spent four thousand dollars to build an addition, including the turret on the corner that gave the building its present look. Before Prohibition, the eatery was known as the Anscheutz Restaurant. A 1969 *Post-Dispatch* article on the restaurant offered this observation by writer Ron Powers about then-owner Nick Laskaris: "Legends that cast Pelican's as a one-time speakeasy abound, but Laskaris denies knowledge of any such thing, deadpan." It is known more definitely what happened in the back of the restaurant during the 1920s. The Lami Real Estate Co. rented that area to the Famous Players Corp. for an open-air movie theater.

In 1938, Pelican became the owner and hired the chef who would develop the restaurant's distinctive menu. Thomas Pisani, who later became part-owner, prepared specialties including fillet of sole, potato pancakes, sauerbraten, stuffed deviled crabs, and stewed chicken and dumplings. Turtle soup, however, stood at the top of the list. The soup—filled with vegetables, spices, and wine—remained a favorite of the restaurant's patrons after Laskaris leased it in 1956. "A cup of turtle soup, prepared in the Pelican's kitchen in a two-day process and emerging thick, dark and succulent, is a good starter," Powers wrote in the 1969 *Post-Dispatch* article about the restaurant. The creator of the soup, Pisani, retired because of poor health in 1974. What went into his soup became an issue after Laskaris gave up his lease in 1975 to devote all his time to the operation of Nico's Restaurant, 5046 Shaw Avenue. He took with him cooks Pisani had trained to prepare the favorite dish. Pisani's widow, Ruby, decided to keep the recipe to herself. "As far as I'm concerned, I'm going to hold onto that secret."

The restaurant opened under new management, Gabriel Shabbaugh. Although Pisani's widow refused to disclose the recipe, Shabbaugh claimed he learned it from a chef Pisani had taught. But the soup itself wasn't enough to keep the place open, and it closed in 1978. The next year, Mayor James Conway cut the ribbon for a new owner, Salim Hanna, who also claimed that a former chef had given him the original recipe. "The one used in the 1950s and 1960s was good," Hanna said. "But I promise you, ours will be better." But, again, it wasn't good enough to keep the place open. Hanna had served authentic Middle Eastern food with the soup before closing in 1982.

Shortly after Hanna shut the place down, a team made up of Charles Dreeba, James Ginther, A. J. Squiteri, and Robert M. Conway pitched in to reopen the place as Paddington and Worthmore's Pelican Café. It featured a menu that included sweet and sour meatballs, steamed shrimp, Kansas City steak, and prime rib. Old articles about the opening don't mention turtle soup. The partners seemed confident enough in their venture that they opened a second location in the old Slay's restaurant at 10203 Gravois Avenue in Affton in 1984. Conway, a redeveloper and former president of Tower Grove Bank and Trust Co., was often seen at both restaurants. Friends described him as friendly and effervescent, but he was hiding a darker side. Family members later told police Conway had been depressed about his business developments. That was how they reacted to the news that Conway set the restaurant on Grand on fire with charcoal briquettes and a flammable liquid early on the morning of June 16, 1985. Then he put a .38-caliber handgun to his head and pulled the trigger. He died late that night. The pelican sign fell into the hands of the city. Today, the sign is owned by the Antique Warehouse, a private museum, which specializes in signs and is located just beyond the boundaries of this book's subject. Different owners have restored the building for offices, but nobody has put a restaurant in it since.

From the Brink

When Ruth Kamphoefner bought a dilapidated Victorian mansion in Lafayette Square in 1970, she noticed some nice ladies walking around the neighborhood. At least they seemed nice to her. In fact, they were prostitutes. Nothing worked in the house, so she had basic plumbing and electrical work done, and replaced broken windows. Then came the rats and roaches. "We worked very fast. We found out the secrets of getting rid of roaches and getting rid of rats," Kamphoefner said. But it was harder to get rid of the rats and roaches who tore down historic houses and wanted to clear the neighborhood to make way for housing projects and a road called the North-South Distributor Highway. But Lafayette Square pioneers like Kamphoefner prevailed, and the neighborhood went on to be one of the prettiest in the South Side.

Kamphoefner told her family's story in *Lafayette Comes Back*, which she self-published in 2000. That story began when her husband suddenly died in 1964, leaving her family living on Social Security checks and her part-time job as an art teacher. Then one day in 1970, she learned a house was available in Lafayette Square for $15,000. It was a much better price than the $35,000 cost of a new three-bedroom house in Affton. So she went looking and found even better bargains. She chose a house at 1526 Mississippi Avenue that was selling for $2,700. "It was pretty bad," said Kamphoefner's daughter, Carol Surgant, who was fourteen when her mother bought the house. "We came into it very naïve about everything." Roaches were especially bad before the family moved in, and they didn't respond to bug spray. Boric acid was more effective. So was a product in a tube called electric paste, but it smelled horrible, Surgant said. "We didn't move down there until we had gotten rid of all the roaches," Surgant said.

When three of the eight rooms were ready, the family moved in and kept fixing up the house. But "ready" for the Kamphoefners didn't mean ready for anybody else. Among other things, there wasn't a kitchen. "For the first year, we cooked on an electric hot plate," Surgant said. "It kind of was like camping out inside a house," she said. Meanwhile, as the five children explored their neighborhood, they found things they wouldn't find in a nicer area. Surgant and a brother found a drunk sleeping in weeds in an empty lot. Men came into the neighborhood looking for prostitutes.

Meanwhile, Kamphoefner worked with others in the community to save the neighborhood. It was lonely work. The main group working to save the neighborhood, the Lafayette Square Restoration Committee, had just enough people to sit around a table, but there were experts, including three engineers and a museum curator. There were enough people to start planting tulips in Lafayette Park. There were enough to fight against the forces that would destroy the neighborhood. In 1972, the Board of Aldermen approved a historic district designation for the neighborhood, which provided protection against demolition of historic buildings and required them to be held to historic standards. The neighbors received more good news in the form of a twenty-five thousand-dollar loan from the National Trust for Historic Preservation to buy historic homes in danger of demolition. The naming of houses in Lafayette Square to the National Register of Historic Places made it more unlikely that a highway would be built through the neighborhood.

With all of this, and the addition of more pioneers, people started seeing major changes, and Kamphoefner kept working for the neighborhood. She sold her first home in 1983 and kept buying. Altogether, she bought eighteen homes in danger of demolition and resold them without a profit. She completely restored seven properties. She lived in a home on Preston Place until 2007, when she moved to a senior citizens apartment in Shrewsbury. Today, she still returns to work on gardens in Lafayette Park. Looking back, Kamphoefner said she never became discouraged. "I think we were optimists all the time," she said. "I would do it again. If I were physically able to, I would do it again." Surgant has similar thoughts. "It was great. I'm glad I did that as a kid rather than living in suburbia."

LAFAYETTE ☆SQUARE☆

The Wayward Steeple

The near South Side's skyline is littered with an army of steeples. One steeple in particular has risen above the rest. For more than one hundred years, people have known there was something grand about St. Francis de Sales Catholic Church. With a three-hundred-foot-tall steeple, the church at 2653 Ohio Avenue is a landmark on Gravois Avenue. After it was dedicated in 1908, it was a fitting replacement for a church demolished in the Great Cyclone of 1896. It was well beyond anything seven German immigrant dairymen could have imagined in 1867 when they bought a tract at Gravois and Ohio for a new parish that would become St. Francis de Sales. Designed to match a Gothic church in Germany, the building contains a 50-foot-tall high altar and a 130-foot-long aisle. The church interior is filled with Gothic arches and stained glass windows. It looked magnificent when seven to nine thousand families were part of a largely German-American parish. It kept that magnificence when attendance at Sunday Mass dropped to fifty or sixty, forcing the parish to close in 2005.

The parish doors being closed were only part of the church's problems. The building held a secret. A four-foot-deep concrete foundation, in poor condition, rests on soil beneath the much-admired steeple. The builders may have thought the foundation was sufficient, but in time, ever so slightly, the steeple started to move. No, the spire isn't in danger of crashing onto Gravois. The slow twist has shifted the spire only a fraction of an inch to the southeast, but it was enough to send cracks throughout the rest of the building. In the choir lofts, cracks developed that were at least a half-inch wide. Temporary repairs ensured that water can't get into the building. A stained glass window near the crack was removed in December 2009 after it bowed several inches toward the inside of the choir loft. Temporary repairs of the cracks kept water and the elements out. Permanent repairs, however, must wait until someone fixes the foundation. Without that fix, the church's long-term structural integrity is in danger, and when the parish closed, it seemed that no group or individual would be able to spearhead those repairs.

Then, at the same time the parish closed, St. Louis Archbishop Raymond Burke did something that brought a new congregation to St. Francis de Sales and new hope for the steeple. He made a request to the Institute of Christ the King Sovereign Priest, a church body dedicated to the traditional Latin Mass. He asked the group to establish St. Francis de Sales as a place to celebrate that Mass. Instead of a parish, set up on geographical lines, it would be an oratory, where anyone could come. Today, there are two Masses each Sunday, drawing a combined total of about a thousand faithful. "Some people come only once a month. They drive up to three hours," said Canon Michael K. Wiener, rector at St. Francis de Sales. Repairs have been done on much of the oratory's campus, which includes two school buildings, a gym, a convent, a rectory, a vacant building, and the church. A charter school, the Knowledge Is Power Program (KIPP) Inspire Academy operates on the church campus. The convent is being restored, and another building is being used by homeschoolers, a day care, and several choirs.

Now the St. Francis de Sales Oratory is looking ahead to the major task of repairing the steeple. An engineering firm determined in 2005 that a rock formation on which to lay a foundation was twenty feet below the ground. A problem was getting underneath to attach the new foundation to the old one. A contractor was selected who could do the work for $1.5 million. The oratory hopes to raise the money for the steeple tower before it turns to future work to preserve the exterior and interior. However, the congregation is young and not big enough to provide the money, Wiener said, but he has faith it will happen.

Sports on a Sunday Morning

A chance discussion over beer at a South Side bar on Labor Day 1944 affected more than ten thousand boys and girls who played youth sports for the next half-century. Oddly, those who were at Becker's Tavern weren't thinking about youth sports at all. They were talking about the soccer and baseball games a group of men had played since the 1920s in the Sunday Morning League at Carondelet Park. Then one of them, Earl Kessler, asked, "Why don't we enter a team in the Muny League?" That discussion led to the formation of the new Carondelet Sunday Morning Athletic Club (CSMAC) to put a team in the citywide Muny League. At first, the group provided a place for men to play baseball and soccer. It bought a building at 1012 Loughborough Avenue in 1946. Different buildings at that address would be at the center of the organization's work for the next sixty years, but then CSMAC branched out, and its efforts truly became memorable. CSMAC is most remembered for its work with a junior group open to boys and girls from ages ten to eighteen. Some time around 1960, the group ceased to be a vehicle for men's sports. Instead, until after 2000, the group gave boys and girls a place to play baseball, softball, soccer, and basketball.

Fifty Years of Sporting Excellence—1944–1994: The C.S.M.A.C. Story was published by the Carondelet Sunday Morning Athletic Club in 1994. "The boys' parents did not have to be a member of C.S.M.A.C.," the book said of those eligible to join the junior group. "All the boys needed was his parents' approval and a dollar bill for his yearly dues. Ten cents a month was acceptable if a dollar was unavailable." That requirement also was waived if necessary. "The dollar dues' only purpose was to provide the boy with a feeling of belonging." But over time, the club shrank as interest and

volunteers declined and young people moved out of the area. In the end, a small group kept the gym open for bingo games that supported the club.

"We had one soccer team and one softball team, and we decided that we would close the doors," said Rich Meisemann, a longtime official of the group. "CSMAC served its purpose. We took care of kids when they couldn't afford to play sports." So in 2005, the club sold its gym building and its eleven acres of property at 1012 Loughborough to the developers of a new shopping center to be called the Loughborough Commons. The club is gone, but the CSMAC lives on in displays at the Carondelet Historical Society, 6303 Michigan Avenue, and in college scholarships from nearly $1 million the group received for the building. "We wanted to keep the name of CSMAC going, and we thought the best way to do that was to give scholarships," Meisemann said. In the five years after the group sold the building, it gave students in area high schools thirty scholarships for sports, academics, and community service worth nearly $300,000. Such is the end of a group that started by charging children a dime a month to play sports.

The American Dream

Fati Dime is living the American dream. A refugee from Mauritania, she is building a life for herself and three of her six children at her Cisse's Fashion and Hair Braiding Salon at 4412 Chippewa Street. She also hopes to bring her three other children over to America, but like many others striving for the American dream, it comes with a cost. "I work twenty-four hours a day. You don't go anywhere. You just work," she said. "The good thing is if you work hard, you can get a lot of opportunities." Dime, who came to America in 2001, received help and training from the International Institute of St. Louis to set up her business.

The agency, which is based at 3654 South Grand Boulevard, has been helping immigrants and refugees adjust to life in St. Louis for more than ninety years. The group was founded in 1919 to help the flood of women who came to the St. Louis area primarily from European countries ravaged by World War I. Then as now, it offered services such as translation, English language classes, meeting medical needs, and helping people find employment. During World War II, the group helped relocate Japanese Americans from interment camps in the Western United States. After the war, it started helping war brides from Japan and Europe. Since then, the focus has changed. In 1954, the agency offered the first citizenship classes in St. Louis to Japanese who were finally able to apply for U.S. citizenship after fifty-year-old restrictions were lifted. In the 1950s and 1960s, it worked with refugees fleeing from the failed Hungarian and Czechoslovakian revolutions. It helped to resettle Vietnamese refugees after the fall of Saigon in 1975 and Bosnians from 1993 to 2001. By the end of 2011, it will have sponsored twenty thousand refugees since 1975.

"We're sort of their Welcome Wagon," said Agency President and CEO Anna Crosslin. The group picks up refugees at the airport, helps them find housing, teaches them English, and helps them find jobs. Many of them since have started businesses that have brought major changes to the South Side. She notes that a primary example of the effect of the agency's help on the community came after the International Institute moved to 3800 Park Avenue near Cardinal Glennon Hospital in 1982.

Vietnamese clients who resettled south of the office along South Grand Boulevard noticed all the boarded-up buildings on South Grand. Others saw hopeless blight. The Vietnamese saw opportunity in an area with affordable rents. Soon they were opening businesses on South Grand. That was the start of the thriving international business district on South Grand south of Arsenal Street. Crosslin sees the same thing happening on Gravois Avenue in the Bevo Mill neighborhood, where Bosnians have brought new life to an area that once was devoid of promise.

Out of the approximately seventy thousand Bosnian refugees and their children now in the area, about half of those live in the city, Crosslin said. The International Institute resettled about seven thousand of them here, while Catholic Charities of the Archdiocese of St. Louis resettled several thousand more. "The anchor resettlements attracted friends and families who had been resettled in other states around the United States when they learned of the opportunities in St. Louis to find jobs and buy affordable homes. They flocked to our communities," Crosslin said. "It's a very typical pattern of immigrant waves throughout history."

Altogether, Crosslin estimates, about 10 percent of the city's population is made up of refugees. Without the help the International Institute provided, "They would basically be dropped in the middle of nowhere, as many of our grandparents and great-grandparents were in earlier generations," Crosslin said. "Instead, within a relatively short period of time, months, not years, most refugees adjust. They can be working, paying taxes, and on their way to integrating and becoming good neighbors, small business owners, and otherwise fully participating and contributing Americans." If anyone wonders how the South Side has turned around so much in recent years, a big reason has to be the hard work of refugees and immigrants. And the International Institute is a big reason why they've succeeded.

THE INTERNATIONAL ✪ INSTITUTE ✪

Raise a Glass

Few lovers of Budweiser, Bud Light, or Michelob have heard the name George Schneider, but perhaps they should raise a glass to him. If it wasn't for George Schneider, they might be drinking Coors or Miller instead. Who knows? In this alternate universe, Anheuser-Busch might be selling soap instead of beer. Schneider played a crucial role in the beginning of this most important of South Side companies. He was a brewer, but not a particularly successful one, which is a key to the story. Likely, he operated the Washington Brewery at 54 S. Third Street in the 1840s and early 1850s, along with a beer garden and a saloon. In 1852, he opened the Bavarian Brewery on the east side of Carondelet Avenue (now South Broadway) between Dorcas and Lynch streets. Soldiers at the nearby U.S. Arsenal provided a plentiful source of customers, so many, in fact, that the company moved to the west side of Eighth Street, between Crittendon and Pestalozzi streets in 1856. Then, perhaps because of the Panic of 1857, he started having money problems and sold his business. The new owners, Hammer & Urban, did well, but fell behind on loans. So in 1860, the firm transferred ownership to a major creditor: the soap and candle manufacturer Eberhart Anheuser.

Anheuser and a friend, the pharmacist William D'Oench, took over the brewery and renamed it the E. Anheuser and Company Bavarian Brewery. Anheuser recognized that while everybody needs soap, what the city's growing population of German immigrants really wanted was beer. He tried without success to manage his soap and beer business in tandem. Eventually, he sought out someone to manage his beer business. "Eberhart wanted a man who knew beer, who loved beer, and who could brew and sell beer," said the self-serving *Making Friends Is Our Business: 100 Years of Anheuser-Busch*, by Roland Krebs with Percy J. Orthwein. So he turned to his son-in-law, Adolphus Busch.

Adolphus was born on July 10, 1839, in the Grand Dutchy of Hesse and immigrated to the United States in 1857. "Having completed his education in Germany, and become a linguist of considerable skill, he went to America to seek his fortune," *Making Friends Is Our Business* claimed. He came to St. Louis and worked as a clerk in the wholesale supply business. Then he went into business with Ernst Wattenberg in the wholesale commission house of Wattenberg, Busch and Co. Somewhere along the line, possibly in business dealings with Anheuser, he met Eberhart's daughter, Lilly. Meanwhile, Adolphus's brother Ulrich met Lilly's sister Anna. On March 17, 1861, Adolphus married Lilly, and Ulrich married Anna, in a double wedding ceremony. "Adolphus was twenty minutes late for the ceremony," Peter Hernon and Terry Ganey wrote in *Under the Influence: The Unauthorized Story of the Anheuser-Busch Dynasty*. On his way to his wedding, he stopped to close a business deal.

After the wedding, Adolphus enlisted in the Union Army for three months. He returned to run his supply business and was taken into Anheuser's business as a partner in 1865. Soon he sold his interest in Wattenberg, Busch and Co. and bought D'Oench's share of the brewery. With the help of Adolphus, the company soon had to increase capacity to twenty-five thousand barrels. Adolphus was using all of his skills to sell his product. The beer was terrible, Hernon and Ganey wrote. To push it, Adolphus offered free beer to customers and payments to bar owners who stocked the beer. He also was early in using pasteurization to preserve the beer and ship it elsewhere.

His biggest innovation, however, was the King of Beers. Brewed with a process similar to the German pilsner beer, the Budweiser lager was introduced by E. Anheuser Co.'s Brewing Association in 1876. But there were problems. The bottler and distributor of the beer, C. Conrad and Co., registered the trademark for Budweiser in 1878. In 1883, Conrad filed for bankruptcy and licensed the name to what had become known as the Anheuser-Busch Brewing Association. In 1891, the brewery acquired all rights to the name in the United States, but disputes continue to this day. Budejovichy Budvar, which started brewing in 1895 in what is now the Czech Republic, also makes a beer called Budweiser. The Czech brewer disputes the rights to the name on the grounds that Budweiser is a style of beer based on the area it came from. Unquestionably, the product sold by Anheuser-Busch, or Anheuser-Busch InBev, since A-B was swallowed up in 2008, is the bigger seller.

RIVER STEAMERS DRI

THEIR MOORINGS.

★ EVENTS ★

The Grand Viaduct

A 1930 city map looks pretty much like a city map today, with a few
exceptions. Among the differences in the 1930 map were the large tracts
of undeveloped land in southwest St. Louis City, particularly the part west
of Hampton Avenue and south of Eichelberger Street. Development in
South St. Louis was delayed primarily because of access to the rest of the
city. South Siders could get downtown without much of a problem, but
east-west railroads and the Mill Creek Valley made it harder for them to
go north. "South Siders had this kind of separate identity from the rest
of the city because they were isolated," said Mark Abbott, a Tower Grove
South resident and a history professor specializing in urban topics at
Harris-Stowe State University. This isolation during its formative years
contributes to the area's unique character.

A change came in 1889, with the construction of the Grand Avenue Viaduct over the railroad tracks in the Mill Creek Valley. When it was built,
the suspension bridge was considered one of the biggest of its kind: seven
hundred feet long and sixty feet wide, with a thirty-six-foot roadway. The
bridge, which was just north of Chouteau Avenue, looked like a smaller
version of the Brooklyn Bridge, which was completed just six years earlier.
As the Brooklyn Bridge connected Manhattan with Brooklyn, the Grand
Viaduct connected the northern and southern parts of St. Louis. David R.
Francis, who then was mayor, said it provided "additional modes of com-
munication between those sections of the city separated by the Mill Creek
Valley and its network of railroad yards." Francis thought the need was so
great that he also wanted one to the east at Twenty-First Street.

Francis didn't get what he wanted, but the Grand Viaduct nonetheless
had a positive effect. "Until that bridge was built, very little development
took place along that South Grand corridor either east or west," said Esley
Hamilton, architectural historian for the St. Louis County Department
of Parks and Recreation. In time, other north-south connections went up
and the old ones became outdated. People complained the Grand Viaduct
wasn't wide enough for all the traffic. In 1960, the old bridge was demolished, and an eighteen-month project started to replace it with a new

six-lane roadway. To mark the occasion, the preservationist Landmarks Association of St. Louis placed a memorial wreath on the old viaduct. Landmarks President Gerhardt Kramer said the wreath was a symbol of regret that it had to be demolished. Kramer emphasized that his group didn't think the old rusty bridge should be preserved. "It is inadequate for present-day traffic," he said. By the time the viaduct became outdated, people well knew about the bottlenecks that a two-lane connector between the north and south caused, but nobody remembered what it was like when there were no connections at all.

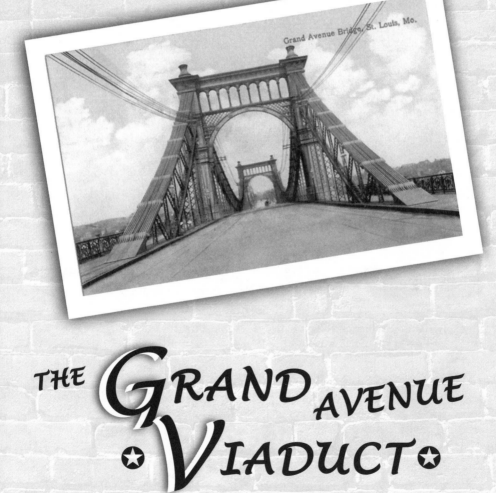

THE GRAND AVENUE ✪VIADUCT✪

A Wound Long to Heal

In terms of numbers, the killer tornado that roared through St. Louis and East St. Louis on May 27, 1896, was the third-most deadly in American history. The monster twister killed 255 people, injured 1,000, and caused—adjusting for inflation—the greatest dollar amount of damage of any tornado in U.S. history. Starting near the current location of the St. Louis Psychiatric Rehabilitation Center on Arsenal Street, the twister struck the Missouri Botanical Garden and sped through Chouteau Avenue, Soulard, and south of downtown. The tornado damaged part of an approach to the Eads Bridge before crossing the river and sinking riverboats and destroying major parts of East St. Louis.

Builders got busy and repaired the damage, but one part of the South Side took well over seventy years to recover. Stately Lafayette Square already was in decline before the cyclone. The richest of St. Louis's rich, who had bought up homes around Lafayette Park after the Civil War, already were pushing further west toward Vandeventer Place, and later the Central West End, to escape the encroaching pollution of the city's factories.

Then came the killer tornado, which made a direct hit on Lafayette Park and the surrounding homes. Everywhere, trees were pulled up and made into splinters. The statues of George Washington and Thomas Hart Benton remained upright amidst the rubble. The Lafayette Park Presbyterian, Methodist, and Baptist churches were gutted, as was nearby City Hospital. The Music Pavilion, a favorite place to hear Strauss waltzes, was destroyed, along with numerous mansions. Charles Gibson, an early resident who served as solicitor general of the United States

THE GREAT of 1896 ⚬CYCLONE⚬

under President Abraham Lincoln, said with tears that he easily could rebuild his home. But he would never live the decades it would take to restore the trees that now were gone from Lafayette Square.

Much of the damage was repaired, but the soul was gone from the place. Soon, the first of the beautiful homes around Lafayette Park was converted into rooming houses and subdivided into multiple dwellings. Then in 1923, the Missouri Supreme Court ruled unconstitutional a zoning law limiting property fronting the park to residences. Grocery stores and service stations went up in place of once-proud homes. Slumlords and criminals took over.

Hope reinvigorated Lafayette Square. At the end of the 1960s, people who believed the former glory could return started buying old property around the park and restoring it. They formed the Lafayette Square Restoration Committee in 1969 and held its first of what has become an annual house tour the next year. In 1972, the Board of Aldermen passed an ordinance making Lafayette Square the city's first historic district. It included limits on demolition of houses and strict restrictions meant to ensure that renovations met historic guidelines. The law provided protection for a new generation of urban pioneers. With their vision and work, Lafayette Square finally was over the Great Cyclone of 1896.

When Beer Flowed Again

After thirteen long, dry years, South Siders raised the biggest glasses they could find after midnight on April 7, 1933. At night clubs, restaurants, and watch parties, they tapped beer mugs filled high with 3.2 percent Budweiser and Falstaff and said to one and all, "Here's to ya'," and "I'm sure glad that's over." Actually, Prohibition wasn't over. That would come on December 5, 1933, when passage of the Twenty-first Amendment repealed Prohibition for all forms of alcohol. But for local beer drinkers and brewers, the passage of the Cullen-Harrison Act was a good start. The law, which took effect April 7, legalized the sale of 3.2 percent alcohol by volume beer and wine in the District of Columbia and the twenty states in which state laws didn't prohibit its sale.

It was reason to celebrate, and South Siders did. About twenty-five thousand people jammed around the Anheuser-Busch plant at Broadway and Arsenal Street. People standing shoulder to shoulder on Pestalozzi Street north of the plant cut off traffic. Inside the brewery, Anheuser-Busch was preparing to ship forty-five thousand cases and eighteen thousand half-barrels right after it became legal. A brass band kept the crowd happy as they awaited the blowing of a whistle at midnight. "When the whistle blew, there was a deafening outburst of cheering," the *Globe-Democrat* said in that morning's edition. "Before the cheering subsided, the great doors of the bottling plant were lifted and the first trucks rolled out, the police clearing a way for them." Among the fifty-five trucks was a light truck under police escort with a case of beer for President Roosevelt and fifty-seven cases for other government officials. They headed for Lambert Field for a flight to Washington. The brewery had sixteen freight cars loaded on switching tracks. Trucks were lined up four blocks long. Meanwhile, a crowd estimated at ten thousand lined up at the Falstaff Brewery on Forest Park Boulevard.

At Anheuser-Busch, KMOX broadcast the words of company Vice President August A.

(Gussie) Busch Jr., in opening ceremonies after midnight. "April the 7th is here and it is a real occasion for thankfulness marking a newfound freedom for the American people made possible by the wisdom, foresight and courage of a great president and the cooperation of an understanding Congress," Busch said. "Out of confusion and anxiety has grown a beacon light to guide the way to better times. Happy, grateful men are back at work after what seems an endless idleness."

The next day, as people recovered from their first legal binge in thirteen years, both Anheuser-Busch and Falstaff were overwhelmed with orders. Phone lines into both breweries were so tied up that it was impossible to get through. While upstarts like Blatz pushed their products in smaller ads, it was up to Falstaff and Anheuser-Busch to brag about themselves in full-page ads. "Prosit!" said a Falstaff ad. "Drink to this joyous advent, a beer of old, that always has been and is today the choicest product of the brewers' art." Anheuser-Busch claimed in its ads that something more than beer was back, but an important part of the economy. "Hands long idle find new jobs. Faces empty of hope brighten to a new promise. Thousands upon thousands find honorable employment." Indeed, some people did go back to work, but it was hardly enough to end the Depression. At least now, though, people could drink away their worries about the economy without worrying about being arrested.

The Choicest Product Goes Bust

It was a typically American story of boom and bust, and much of it played itself out on the South Side. In the 1950s and 1960s, St. Louis's Falstaff beer challenged Anheuser-Busch for dominance in the St. Louis market and became one of the leading brewers in the country. Then a slide began, and the company disappeared. So ended a tradition that began when the William J. Lemp Brewery, based at Lemp Avenue and Cherokee Street, introduced the brand at the start of the twentieth century. After the onset of Prohibition, the Lemp Brewery sold the company's trademark for twenty-five thousand dollars to a company organized by brewer Joseph Griesedieck and his son Alvin. It seemed foolish, but "Papa Joe" Griesedieck had no doubts. "He was convinced that eventually Prohibition would be repudiated by the American public and real beer would come back," Alvin Griesedieck wrote in his 1951 book, *The Falstaff Story*.

The Falstaff Corp. endured Prohibition by selling a nonalcoholic beer called Hek, along with other products like root beer, ham, and bacon. When Prohibition ended in 1933 Falstaff quenched thirsty beer drinkers throughout the country. The Falstaff Corp. received hundreds of applications from throughout the country from franchisers ready to sell the brew. The first truckloads moved out of a brewery at 3662–84 Forest Park Boulevard on April 7, 1933. That plant stayed open until 1958. In the South Side, another plant opened at the end of Prohibition at 3181 Michigan Avenue and remained open until 1952. A plant at 2000 Madison Street operated from 1948 to 1967. Meanwhile, Griesedieck Brothers Brewery, started by Joseph's brother Henry in 1911, also turned out Griesedieck Brothers Beer from a brewery at Shenandoah and Lemp. The beer sponsored Cardinals games from 1944 to 1953, a time when Harry Caray first broadcast here. Falstaff merged with Griesedieck Brothers Brewery in 1957 and immediately killed production of that brand. It produced Falstaff at that plant from 1957 to 1977.

The merger was one of the moves that helped to bring Falstaff close to the front of the brewing pack in the 1950s. By the end of the 1950s, Falstaff beer, "the Choicest Product of the Brewer's Art," was briefly the third-most-popular beer in America. In 1963, the *Globe-Democrat* reported on the busy life of Marie Olliges, who was responsible for furnishing Falstaff office buildings in eight different cities: St. Louis, Omaha, New Orleans, San Jose, Chicago, Fort Wayne, Galveston, and El Paso. The company had an impressive-looking headquarters at 5050 Oakland Avenue. It bragged about itself at the Falstaff Museum of Brewing in the Falstaff Inn at Shenandoah Avenue and Salena Street, near the brewery at Shenandoah and Lemp.

But the good times couldn't last. Production peaked in 1966 and then started to slide. In 1970, the company omitted a quarterly dividend to stockholders. In 1975, San Francisco businessman Paul Kalmanovitz bought the firm and moved its headquarters to San Francisco. The office at 5050 Oakland Avenue closed. Falstaff reintroduced Griesedieck Brothers Beer briefly in the mid-1970s, but sales floundered. In 1977, the brewery on Shenandoah closed. Sales plummeted. The product was kept alive, but the company sold a mere 1,468 barrels in 2004. The next year, owner Pabst Brewing Co. of San Antonio, turned off the tap on Falstaff for good. Today, the Saint Louis Science Center occupies the Oakland Avenue property where Falstaff had its headquarters. The office on Oakland was demolished to make way for the Saint Louis Science Center. The site of the brewery on Michigan Avenue now has a shuttered auto repair place on it. In 2006, a company announced plans to develop the old Falstaff brewery at Lemp and Shenandoah as Falstaff Heights, complete with condominiums, stores, restaurants, and light industry. Nothing came of the plan, and the brewery is empty. A title loan company now occupies the old Falstaff Inn nearby.

In their book *St. Louis Brews: 200 Years of Brewing in St. Louis, 1809–2009*, Henry Herbst, Don Roussin, and Kevin Kious offer several reasons for Falstaff's demise. Among them were a change to the formula that the public didn't like and the age and inefficiency of the company's plants. A big money-draining loser was the Tapper, a small aluminum barrel that contained a case of beer. Each cost the company forty-eight dollars. The one-dollar deposit was hardly enough to persuade buyers to bring them back. "The bottom line is that Falstaff simply could not sell enough beer or limit production costs sufficiently to survive the beer wars that took place in the 1970s and beyond," *St. Louis Brews* claimed. For all of that, there are plenty of people who still hanker for one more drink of that choicest product: Falstaff.

The Great St. Louis Bank Robbery

It was the stuff you'd see in a 1950s crime flick. A perfectly planned bank robbery goes awry. Crowds of police officers and onlookers gather as terrified bank customers and employees crouch down to avoid the gunfire. When the shooting stops, a police officer is injured, two bank robbers are dead, and one robber is injured. The getaway car's driver eludes police but is quickly caught. In the best movie style, one robber takes his own life after declaring police would never take him alive. A police officer kills another robber as the thief rushes to the front door while using a woman as a shield. In fact, these sequences were the subject of a movie, based on actual events that occurred on April 24, 1953. The robbery at Southwest Bank at South Kingshighway Boulevard and Southwest Avenue was to become known as the Great St. Louis Bank Robbery.

The mastermind of the heist was Fred William Bowerman, described by the *Globe-Democrat* as a "lean, hard-eyed 'crime specialist' who was trading shots with police as far back as 1932." The year before, he was one of the robbers who shot a bank employee and got away with a total of $53,000 in the robbery of the National Bank and Trust Company of South Bend, Indiana. Now he was on the FBI's Ten Most Wanted List. Bowerman assembled his gang in Chicago and told members to "forget" their names and live apart from each other. That way, they couldn't tell police about the others if they were captured. Before the robbery, they met in Tower Grove Park to go over final details.

The robbery began at 10:15 on a payday Friday morning, when the bandits burst into the bank with cloths tied over the lower parts of their faces. One of them, holding a sawed-off shotgun and a brown zipper bag, jumped to a counter where he could see everybody in the bank. "This is a holdup. Everybody stand still," he shouted. He turned to the tellers and said, "Come out of those cages and get down on the floor." In another part of the building, the bank's directors were in their weekly meeting. Hearing the commotion, Bank President Dillon J. Ross called the switchboard operator who was working in the basement and told her to call the police. Meanwhile, a teller pressed a button under a counter alerting authorities.

Corporal Robert Heinz and Patrolman Melburn
Stein were quick to respond. The robbers answered
Stein's shots with gunfire. Heinz was shot in his ear
and neck. Soon police from throughout the city
were on the scene. As customers and bank employees cowered on the floor, police tossed tear gas
canisters through the bank's windows. Bowerman
grabbed Eva Hamilton and pressed his sawed-off
shotgun against her back. "Don't shoot, or I'll kill
her," he said. Undeterred, Stein aimed from the hip
and felled the bandit. Bowerman later died from

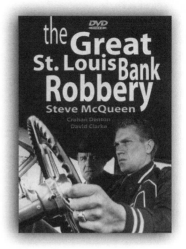

his wounds. "I felt sure I could get him by shooting from the hip and not
harm the woman," Stein later said. "I had eight years of training in the Marine Corps in shooting from the hip." The game was up, and robber Frank
Vito knew it. "They're not going to get me. I'll kill myself first," he said. He
put a pistol to his head and shot himself. Another robber, William Scholl,
grabbed bank customer Gloria Cantino. "Don't shoot. I've got a baby at
home," she pleaded. "Don't worry, lady, I won't hurt you. I've got children of
my own," Scholl responded. Wounded by a shot fired by police, Scholl gave
himself up at Cantino's urging. Several days later, police arrested the driver
of the getaway car, former Marquette University football player Glenn
Chernick, in Chicago. On the floor of the bank, police found a bag the
robbers had stuffed with nearly $141,000. Chernick and Scholl later were
sentenced to twenty-five years in prison.

St. Louis police received praise from throughout the country for the way
they'd foiled the robbery. One, Stein, had a chance to show the world how
he did it, by playing himself in a movie about the heist called *The Great
St. Louis Bank Robbery*. The 1959 movie starred a new actor named Steve
McQueen. The director was Charles Guggenheim, who went on to win
three Academy Awards for his documentaries. The movie featured shots
of Southwest Bank and other South Side locations. But it's not a travel-
ogue. Those and other scenes are shot in a gloomy black and white that
befits a tale of a sad group of criminals about to do something stupid.
McQueen wasn't yet the actor who rode a motorcycle in *The Great Escape*,
but he did show promise as a college dropout showing doubts about the
robbery plan.

When the South Side Got Famous

Southtown Famous brought class to the South Side. Long before Macy's bought the parent company of Famous-Barr, the department store was the city's equivalent of Macy's. After Famous opened a $3.25 million branch at Chippewa Street and Kingshighway Boulevard on August 24, 1951, South Side families didn't have to take the Chevy or the bus downtown to buy fancy suits and dresses they saw advertised in the paper.

The store opened to big fanfare. Fifteen thousand people showed up to watch Mayor Joseph M. Darst use specially made sterling silver scissors to cut the ribbon opening the store. Seven-year-old Patricia and nine-year-old Susan Feiner, granddaughters of Famous-Barr Vice President Fred Z. Salomon, dressed in navy blue and white polka dot costumes to hold the ribbon for the mayor to cut. Explorers and Boy Scouts from Troop 115 from nearby St. Mary Magdalen Church provided the color guard. A crew from KSD-TV (now KSDK-TV) showed up to film the event for the six o'clock news. Darst spoke with enthusiasm about the store's possibilities. "I believe this beautiful structure signifies the confidence held by business leaders throughout the nation in the people of St. Louis," the *Globe-Democrat* quoted him as saying. "Here we have an outstanding example of this company's recognition of the economic possibilities to be developed in St. Louis." The crowd was so big that twice in the first twenty minutes after the doors opened store officials asked the police to close them.

The next day, the *Globe-Democrat* quoted Morton D. May, Famous-Barr general manager and president of May Department Stores Company, on the importance of the store. He said the company's growth was closely connected with the expansion of the city. He spoke of the enormous development of the south and west parts of the city, which the store would serve. The store actually was the second Famous-Barr opened outside of downtown. The first was in Clayton. But what the Southtown Famous had to offer made up for the fact that it wasn't first. Shoppers could choose from 150 different departments. Two thousand cars could fit into fifteen acres of parking lots. Motorists who parked in a lot across Chippewa

Street could enter the store through a tunnel leading under the busy road. Not wanting to waste any chances, the store lined the tunnel with kiosks.

In 1959, shoppers could view new gas appliances in a seven-room land-scaped house in a parking lot called the "Blue Flame Home." A beer garden went up in 1966. Until the early 1970s, people filled the tunnel before the store opened on the last Thursday of every month to be the first inside for the "Dollar Day" promotion. Frank Scheithauer, a South Sider and a longtime Southtown display manager, noted in a 1995 article in the *South Side Journal* that window displays changed every two weeks. "We were real elaborate with the windows," he said. "It took a day and a half at the most to do one window, but sometimes we had to do three or four in a day."

It was a place to make memories, but it couldn't last. Faced with a loss of customers, Famous-Barr closed the store in January 1992. Plans were to replace it with a new Home Quarters mega hardware store. Nothing came of that, and a wide coalition of neighborhood groups fought plans to put a K-Mart in its place. They won, and a combination of small and big stores opened at the location in the mid-2000s as the Southtown Centre. The center, which includes such stores as Starbucks, PetSmart, Walgreens, and OfficeMax, is one of a number of shopping areas that are thriving on the South Side. They include Target, Hampton Village, Loughborough Commons, the South Grand international business district, and a number of smaller neighborhood shopping districts.

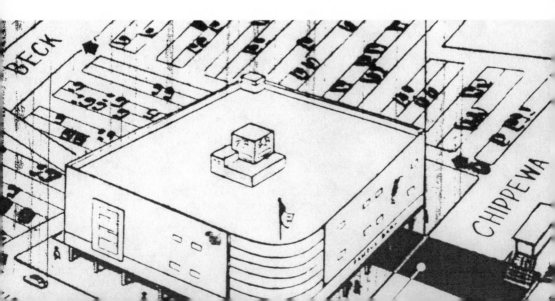

A Monster Strikes

As the city slept early the morning of February 10, 1959, a deadly beast prepared to pounce. At Lambert–St. Louis Airport, meteorologists read their thermometers and barometers and saw something was wrong. The temperature dropped while air pressure spiked. Earlier, they had warned of severe thunderstorms, but nothing more. A squall line had developed about eight to ten miles long moving about sixty miles ahead of a cold front going east at about thirty to thirty-five miles an hour. Then it happened. "Apparently the frontal cloud touched down and made contact," Weather Bureau meteorologist Leon Greninger told the *Post-Dispatch* later.

That's the way a meteorologist would say that the third most deadly tornado in St. Louis history met the earth around 1:40 a.m. at Manchester Avenue and Brentwood Boulevard and roared northeast. The 694-foot-tall tower of KTVI-Channel 2 at 5915 Berthold Avenue crumbled and fell onto the nearby Arena parking lot and a four-family apartment. The twister then punched a hole in the roof of the Arena, demolished the Old Barn's east ornamental tower, and destroyed nearby homes. Then it crossed Highway 40 and exacted deadly tolls on neighborhoods between Kingshighway and Grand boulevards. As the storm moved on, Cardinals first baseman Joe Cunningham was discussing a Bible verse with a buddy at his apartment at 4255 Olive Street when they heard a roar. "I jumped from my chair and ran into the next room and just then the ceiling caved in where I had been sitting. I crouched in a corner of the next room until we could make our way to the street," he said. While he thanked God

THE GREAT of 1959 TORNADO

for sparing his life, the tornado sputtered out around 2:15 a.m. near the McKinley Bridge. Twenty-one people were dead and 354 injured. The *Globe-Democrat* estimated that four thousand buildings were damaged.

It was deadly, and the Weather Bureau missed it. It didn't issue a "special bulletin" about a tornado until 3:30 a.m. Sheepishly, the bureau, the forerunner of the National Weather Service, contended it didn't issue a warning because the twister was an isolated case that couldn't be pinpointed. Even if it had predicted the tornado, it couldn't have gotten the word out at that late hour, the bureau contended nobody had made arrangements to use the civil defense siren system for that purpose. Meanwhile, the city's civil defense office didn't start work until three hours after the tornado struck. "I grant you the way it did work was all wrong," Retired Brigadier General Francis P. Harding, the city's civil defense director, said. However, the civil defense operation responded enough that Mayor Raymond Tucker praised it for its work after the initial delay. After the deadly tornado in 1927, it would have taken twenty-four to thirty-six hours to organize a disaster response, he said.

Others responded quickly. Overwhelmed by the carnage, the city's hospitals met the challenge. Homer G. Phillips Hospital, located near the worst of the carnage, did well by following a disaster plan it had previously rehearsed. The American Red Cross set up four shelters for storm victims. Within hours, President Dwight D. Eisenhower declared St. Louis a major disaster area, making it eligible for federal relief funds. And TV watchers worried they might not see episodes of *Maverick* and *77 Sunset Strip* were relieved to learn Channel 2 was back on the air with a weak low-powered signal by 4 p.m. Meanwhile, the *Globe-Democrat* tried to calculate when the next big tornado would strike. Major twisters killed 255 people in 1896, 76 in 1927, and 21 in 1959 and came at the rate of once every 31 or 32 years. By that logic, the next giant twister should have been in 1990. It hasn't arrived yet.

The Intruding Interstates

Dwight Eisenhower wreaked havoc, first as a general moving his armies across France and Germany and then as the president who established the Interstate Highway System. Both actions did good, but at a cost. When two interstates came to the South Side, they ended traffic snarls and made it faster to get from downtown to Arnold or Kirkwood. But people who had lived in their homes for decades were uprooted and made to live elsewhere. Neighborhoods were split. If the new Interstates 44 and 55 quickly brought people into the city from Fenton and South County, they also made it easier for city residents to move away. Many did. What happened with the interstates here and elsewhere was an example of the law of unintended consequences.

South Siders first heard of the highways after Eisenhower signed the Federal Aid Highway Act of 1956. In October 1957, news came of plans to spend $47 million on a 15.4-mile I-55 from the Meramec River through South County and into the South Side. Then in 1960, the Missouri Highway Department announced a route for Interstate 44 that generally followed its current path, including through the Hill neighborhood. It didn't make two powerful Hill neighborhood politicians happy. State Representative Paul M. Berra complained the route was two miles longer than other proposed routes. Twenty-Fourth Ward Alderman Anthony Mascazzini contended that the route wouldn't serve the most people. "The route chosen will bring traffic congestion to our ward and to every ward east of us," he said.

As people in the path of I-44 worried, the state started buying property in the path of I-55. An early victim was Cherokee Cave at 3400 South Broadway, which once was used by the old Lemp Brewery to keep beer cool. The historic Chatillon-DeMenil Mansion on the same property was saved when the path of the interstate was moved east. A civic group could purchase it. The Landmarks Association of St. Louis persuaded Union Electric (now AmerenUE) to buy the mansion from the state. Another historic mansion wasn't as fortunate. The Philip Medart House at 1729 Missouri Avenue was sold to the State Highway Commission to make way for I-44. The mansion was built in 1890 by Philip Medart, who was an officer in the Union forces in the Civil War. He later patented a number of inventions, including mechanical devices and pulleys. Another historic house on the same block, the Carl Daenzer Mansion, also was sacrificed for Interstate 44. Daenzer was a prominent German immigrant journalist in St. Louis in the last half of the 1800s.

Even where historic houses weren't sacrificed, there were reasons to worry. In 1965, years before I-44 construction started in their area, people living around Tower Grove Park and the Missouri Botanical Garden expressed concern about what was happening in areas the state had bought. In some sections, the state tore down buildings without clearing away rubble. In other sections, people were allowing their property to deteriorate because they knew the state would buy it. Property bought by the state stayed vacant for months. That way, the state could tear down whole groups of buildings. It was good for the state budget, but not good for neighborhoods.

In the Hill neighborhood, loud and persistent protests forced the builders of I-44 to change their plans not once but twice. They first focused on an interchange planned for Macklind Avenue and I-44. That was too much for Hill residents, who worried the project would take about a third of the popular Berra Park at Macklind and Shaw avenues and remove nine or ten more houses. The neighbors organized trips to the state capital to protest the plans. Before long, the interchange was dropped from the plans for the interstate, but Hill residents weren't done. In the early 1970s, concerned that some Hill residents north of the interstate would be cut off from the rest of the neighborhood, they fought for another bridge across the highway just east of the Macklind Avenue bridge. Hundreds turned out at meetings on the Hill and in Jefferson City to press their case. Neighbors even called on television personality Joe Garagiola, who grew up on the Hill, to intervene on their behalf with his friend, U.S. Secretary of Transportation John Volpe. In the end, the pressure paid off. Hill residents got their Edwards Street overpass. "It shows organizational skill. It shows the very fact that people were determined," said Monsignor Salvatore Polizzi. At the time, he was assistant pastor of the Hill's St. Ambrose Catholic Church and a key leader of the neighborhood's fights over I-44. Their efforts reduced the effect of those projects, but the construction of I-44 and I-55 on the South Side changed neighborhoods forever.

The End of Childhood Memories

It was the Six Flags of its time, and it burned on a hot summer day. The blaze that destroyed the Forest Park Highlands was nearly a half-century ago, but those who remember its passing still grieve for it as the end of a precious childhood memory. They think of the pool they swam in during school picnics, the carousel, the rocket ship, the fun houses, the train, and the kisses they stole from their dates on the Ferris wheel. The amusement park in the 5600 block of Oakland Avenue was a place for making such memories after the Highlands Cottage Restaurant opened there in 1896. A merry-go-round soon went up, followed by nine other rides. School children took the streetcar to the Highlands and delighted in the ever-expanding amusement park.

Over the years, local boxers had a chance to try their skill against traveling champion boxers such as Jack Dempsey and "Gentleman Jim" Corbett. John Philip Sousa directed his band at the Highlands, and stars such as Eddie Howard, Harry James, Tommy Dorsey, Marie Dressler, and Sophie Tucker entertained. At one time, one hundred schools a year booked picnics at the park. Sandy Honaker of Wentzville remembers going to the Highlands when she attended Epiphany of Our Lord School at 6576 Smiley Avenue. "Our school picnics were held at the Highlands. That was a big exciting treat," said Honaker, who lived near present-day Interstate 44 and Arsenal Street until she was eighteen. She recalls "the old wooden roller coasters and all the rides. That was really fun."

People loved the place, but in the early 1960s, the Junior College District, now the St. Louis Community College, coveted the fourteen-acre property for a campus. Rumors spread that 1963 would be the Highlands' last year.

THE FOREST PARK HIGHLANDS

While folks were discussing what might happen with the Highlands, a fire settled the matter. Around 2:30 p.m. on July 19, 1963, a fire broke out in the basement of the building housing the restaurant, concession stands, and dance hall. The flames quickly spread, but by 3 p.m., firefighters thought the fire was under control. Winds, however, kicked up to fifteen to twenty miles an hour. Soon there was nothing firefighters could do. "All the water in the world wouldn't put that out," Assistant Fire Chief Robert Olsen said. "It makes a man feel small and insignificant to watch something like this and to be helpless no matter how many big pieces of equipment you have." The heavy black smoke and fire rose as high as 100 to 150 feet high and could be seen for miles.

When the fire was over, only the roller coaster, Ferris wheel, and carousel survived among the rides. "It was sad. Then we had to take the bus all the way up to the Chain of Rocks for our school picnics," Honaker said. She referred to the old Chain of Rocks Amusement Park near the old Chain of Rocks Bridge. Speculation was that careless smoking or faulty wiring was the cause, but nobody knew for sure. Part of what is now the St. Louis Community College at Forest Park went up on the park property. A question turned up at local trivia nights: "Where did the carousel from the Forest Park Highlands wind up?" Answer: St. Louis County's Faust Park. *St. Louis Post-Dispatch* writer Theodore P. Wagner noted another memory of the park: "Fire spectators observed that the illuminated Star Spangled Banner, high above the park, appeared and reappeared through black clouds of smoke like the flag of a ship sinking with colors flying." Like the original Star Spangled Banner, this one remained when the last of the fire was out.

The Irish Go to the Dogs

A full-blooded Irishman, Bob Corbett has extra reasons to smile every St. Patrick's Day. Since the mid-1990s, Corbett has lived in the house he grew up in on Tamm Avenue in Dogtown. By coincidence or not, that gave him the perfect view of the annual St. Patrick's Day Parade of the Ancient Order of Hibernians. For nearly a quarter-century, the parade has passed in front of his house. The St. Louis City and St. Louis County boards of the Hibernians first held the parade in Clayton on March 17, 1984. Unfortunately, the next year, Clayton insisted on holding it on a Saturday, even though March 17 that year was on a Sunday. So the parade in 1985 was held on March 17, but on Howdershell Road in Hazelwood. Finally, the Hibernians decided to move the parade to Dogtown, which has long had a reputation of being the last traditional Irish neighborhood in St. Louis.

It's not quite true to say Dogtown is an Irish neighborhood, Corbett said. Then again, he adds, it's sort of true. Since around the time he moved into the home he grew up in, the retired philosophy professor at Webster University has become his neighborhood's leading historian. A curious type, he decided the idea that Dogtown was and is an Irish neighborhood should be tested. He looked at all census records from 1900 for people who lived in present-day Dogtown—from Oakland Avenue to Interstate 44 and Macklind to McCausland avenues.

"It turns out that the Irish were not even the dominant minority," Corbett said. Germans outnumbered Irish by about twenty. The Irish outnumbered French by about twenty. Others who followed included English and Croatians. But these numbers don't mean the place wasn't Irish. The dominant social organization of the area was St. James the Greater Catholic Church, which started around 1860 after miners and brick makers started coming to the area in the late 1850s. For ninety-two years, from the time the church started in 1860 to 1952, the church's pastors were born, educated, and ordained in Ireland.

They came to the church as missionary priests, and all made their mark. The last of those Irish pastors, Father Patrick J. O'Connor, wrote about them in his 1937 book, *History of Cheltenham and St. James Parish*. He served forty years at the church, from 1912 until his death in 1952. The church's first pastor, Father John O'Sullivan, who served from 1860 to 1861, was a "hot and outspoken secessionist." Father Thomas Manning, who served from May 1869 to January 31, 1870, left the parish suddenly and was reported to be insane. The most revered and loved of the early pastors was Father Henry Kelly, who served from 1870 to 1878. Of the Reverend Edmond Casey, who was pastor from 1896 and 1916, O'Connor wrote, "He was by no means an ascetic and he was rarely suspected of being saintly, but he prayed with the confidence of a bad little boy that right away forgot and was mischievous." O'Connor also wrote that "His laughter was loud and contagious, his sympathy was deep and tear drops came as quickly to his eye as to a woman's." O'Connor could speak with experience about Casey, since he served under him for four years before he took over the parish.

Those priests were different but were all united in faith and nationality. As Corbett sees it, the uneducated miners and brick makers relied on those priests to teach them how to behave. In response, the priests taught them how to live in an Irish village. "It became Irish culturally, although it was not ethnically. It's maintained a great deal of that today," Corbett said. As for what goes by his house every St. Patrick's Day, he said, "I'm delighted with the parade, utterly totally delighted. Best day of the year."

Father O'Connor poses with children from St. James Parish.

An Exorcism

At hospitals, doctors try to use the science they have learned to cure diseases of the body and mind, but people say something profoundly unscientific happened in 1949 in the since-demolished psychiatric wing of Alexian Brothers Hospital at 3933 South Broadway. There, the accounts say, priests performed a full-blown exorcism on a fourteen-year-old boy complete with weird noises and flying things. The events at the institution now called St. Alexius Hospital later became the basis of a 1971 novel, *The Exorcist*, and an Oscar-winning movie of the same name in 1973. William Peter Blatty, author of both the novel and the screenplay, learned about the exorcism after reading a three-paragraph news article. Blatty, who also wrote scripts for director Blake Edwards, made the person who was exorcised a twelve-year-old girl and located the event in Mount Ranier, Maryland, a suburb of Washington, D.C. His account, including a description of the possessed girl as "a cursing, vomiting, convulsive, murdering monster," led many critics and Catholics to call *The Exorcist* exploitative and harmful.

The real event was scary enough, if the accounts are to be believed. Early in 1949, the fourteen-year-old boy and his grandmother started hearing odd scratching noises for several hours each night in a home in Mount Rainier. About a month later, scratches were seen on the boy's body. Then words began to appear in the scratches. The family, which was Lutheran, asked for help from a Lutheran minister. The Lutheran minister asked for help from a priest. Two priests were injured in an attempt to exorcise the boy at Georgetown University Hospital. One, the Reverend Albert E. Hughes, lost full use of his arm when the boy slashed his right arm with a piece of bedspring. He broke the nose of a second, the Reverend Walter H. Halloran. The boy then was moved to St. Louis where his mother had an uncle and an aunt. The boy wound up at Alexian Brothers, where the Reverend William S. Bowdern, pastor of St. Francis Xavier Church at St. Louis University, was named to lead the exorcism. Others present who assisted were the Reverend William Van Roo and Halloran.

The
Reverend Raymond
Bishop described the events in
detail in a twenty-six-page diary. That diary provided much of the basis for Thomas B. Allen's
1993 book about the events: *Possessed: The True Story of an
Exorcism*. Halloran talked about it in a 1988 newspaper interview. "The
little boy would go into a seizure and get quite violent," Halloran said. "So
Father Bowdern asked me to hold him." The priest also contended arrows,
streaks, and words such as "hell" appeared on the child's skin. The story
was kept quiet for years, but rumors led St. Louis Cardinal Joseph Ritter
to order a Jesuit examiner to conduct an investigation. The investiga-
tor concluded demonic possession wasn't involved, but a "psychosomatic
disorder and some kinesis action that we do not understand but which is
not necessarily preternatural."

Bowdern, meanwhile, never acknowledged his role in the exorcism but
confided to friends he believed it was a bona fide incident of possession. Mickey McTague, a Catholic and well-known local figure who has
made a long study of the events at Alexian Brothers Hospital, agrees
with Bowdern. McTague's father was a close friend of Dr. Ed Sassin, who
was chief of psychiatry at Alexian Brothers at the time of the exorcism.
McTague, who was nine at the time, remembers Sassin talking about the
events when he visited the McTague home at 3128 Allen Avenue in
Compton Heights. Almost all of the nearly fifty witnesses to the event
believed demonic activity was involved, McTague said. What they saw
convinced them that something happened at Alexian Brothers that science could not explain.

A Tale of Twisted Boundaries

Somebody living at the northwest corner of Keokuk Street and Ohio Avenue with a complaint about neighbors across the street may think he'll get help by calling his alderman. Unfortunately, that alderman, Craig Schmid of the 20th Ward, won't be able to help by himself. That's because every other corner of that intersection is in the 9th Ward of Alderman Kenneth Ortmann. Schmid would have to go to Ortmann to get the complaint resolved. There are intersections like that in every ward in St. Louis, but the 20th Ward and the surrounding 9th Ward may have the most in the city. There are more than two-dozen such street corners in the 20th Ward. It didn't just happen. It's all about politics, the lengths politicians take to rid themselves of a pesky politician, and how those things make it tougher for city residents.

In general, the 20th Ward is on either side of Chippewa Street from east of Grand Boulevard to Interstate 55. The actual boundaries are a mess of lines turning back and forth at street corners more than sixty times. It leaves constituents at the edge of the ward scratching their heads about who represents them. "It makes it more difficult than it needs to be," Schmid said. It's also hard for Ortmann. His 9th Ward surrounds the 20th on the north, south, and east. A narrow strip east of Interstate 55 connects the north and south portions. He can't drive from the north part of his ward to the south part without passing through Schmid's ward.

The reason for the confusion is a woman who never lived in the ward, at least where the ward is now. Sharon Tyus, a fiery alderwoman, represented the 20th Ward when it was on the North Side. It still might be on the North Side if she hadn't made enemies, including in Mayor Francis Slay's administration. They found their chance during ward redistricting in 2001. Every ten years, after census figures are in, aldermen draw new boundaries. Since at least 1961, the board frequently has moved a ward from one part of the city to another. Not surprisingly, the wards chosen for those moves are the ones represented by the least powerful or most unpopular alderman. In 2001, Tyus was the one sold down the river.

The 2001 debate over redistricting was the hottest in years. Tyus's polemics were among the most vociferous of the North Side protests against a plan that included moving her ward south and put the number of black aldermen at a dozen, out of twenty-eight members. Schmid's 10th Ward would be moved west to parts of the Hill, Southwest Garden, Tower Grove South, Northampton, and Kings Oak neighborhoods. The 20th Ward was placed where the old 10th Ward had been. But those who drew the ward's map worried about suits by African-Americans claiming they'd been robbed of a ward. So they added zigzag lines to ensure that African-Americans would be in the majority. Schmid expressed his frustration about the redistricting in a December 2001 letter to the Board of Aldermen, "The shapes and relationships of the proposed 9th and 20th Wards as well as the shifting of the 10th Ward location, for example, are so bizarre that they can only be understood as segregating voters on the basis of race—with race predominating to the exclusion of other necessary concerns." He voted "present" on the final vote on the redistricting plan but expressed the hope the mayor would work to improve the new ward. The resulting hodgepodge of jagged lines in the map of the 20th Ward makes it worthy of the word *gerrymandered*.

The plan was approved and went into effect at the beginning of 2002. From then until Schmid faced election in 2003, he represented his old ward and his new ward. For each of those wards, he attended neighborhood meetings, tried to answer gripes about potholes, and introduced bills on behalf of residents. "It's entirely baffling to constituents, because there's an accountability problem," Schmid said. Tyus, meanwhile, lived the fiction that her ward was still up north. She tried to have money allocated to the 20th Ward for purposes like tree planting and sidewalks spent in her old ward. She filed for 20th Ward alderman but was disqualified because she didn't live there. Schmid easily was elected 20th Ward alderman in April 2003. In the same election, bar operator Joseph Vollmer was elected 10th Ward alderman. Things returned to normal, except for the gerrymandered boundary lines. Residents of the ward who ask how the unorthodox boundary came to be are in for a long story about politics, ward maps, and an unpopular alderwoman.

★ UNUSUAL, ★
UNIQUE,
OR JUST
PLAIN ODD

A Brainy Place To Eat

Customers say the fried chicken at Ferguson's Pub is better than Hodak's. But that's not what makes the place at 2925 Mount Pleasant Street stand out. The brains of the operation do. No, that's not Billie Ferguson, the bar's eighty-three-year-old owner. She's smart, too, but it's the fried beef brains served on rye bread with pickles, onions, chips, and horseradish sauce that have brought people all the way from Potosi to try them. A man who lived in the area moved to Washington, D.C., and came back for a visit. He asked for forty of the brain patties—hold the bread, thank you. He put them in dry ice and brought them to Washington, where they don't have brains.

"They taste like scrambled eggs or liver. They're really bland, really mild," the red-haired Ferguson said. They taste like chicken to her son Steve. They look sort of like a breaded pork cutlet and long have been served at a few eateries on the South Side. They've been on the menu at Ferguson's ever since Billie and her husband, John, opened the restaurant on St. Patrick's Day in 1980. There had been a bar at the same place for thirty years before that. "When we bought this, they still walked in and bought those buckets of beer," Ferguson said.

They also bought their share of brain sandwiches there. The pub's brain sandwiches once came in second in a cook-off on the steps of the Old Courthouse downtown. Ferguson thought her sandwiches were the best and asked one of the judges, the legendary 11th Ward Alderman Albert "Red" Villa why they didn't win. "He said, 'You had the best brain sandwich.' I said, 'Why didn't you let me come in first?' He said, 'You're not in my district.'"

Today, Ferguson runs the pub herself, after John died in January 2010. A huge mirror is behind the bar, and red-and-white plaid plastic tablecloths are on the tables. A big framed picture of Mark McGwire smacking a home run is among the items on the wall honoring the Cardinals. There are numerous signs for Anheuser-Busch products, which help wash down many of the fifty or so brain sandwiches sold at the pub each month. Ferguson's customer John Dennis had one once last year. "I thought it was OK until I got to the middle. It's not for me," said Dennis, who does customer support for AT&T. "I didn't feel smarter." A customer who only gave his first name—Brian—said they make the best brain sandwiches at Ferguson's. "I'm going by hearsay," he said. Barb Gannon, a waitress at the place, wouldn't go near the stuff. For those who do like brain sandwiches, they're harder to find. Fewer establishments sell them. Suppliers also don't sell as much. But for those who look and have the stomach for it, there still are places to buy this South Side delicacy.

THE BRAIN SANDWICH

A Blessed Mistake

A mistake in the kitchen more than sixty years ago may have led to a Hill neighborhood specialty that's as much a part of St. Louis's culinary sphere as pork steaks, Gus' Pretzels, and gooey butter cakes. The deep-fried delight, however, has origins shrouded in mystery. Mickey Garagiola, brother of broadcaster Joe Garagiola, contends the mistake happened at Oldani's Tavern, which today is Mama Campisi's Restaurant at 2132 Edwards Street. According to Mickey, some time in the late 1940s an inebriated bartender took an order of ravioli and dropped it in boiling oil instead of boiling water. Rather than waste it, the bar's owner had it served to customers with cheese and red sauce. Garagiola claims he was there after spending the night as a waiter at Ruggeri's Restaurant and saw the new creation brought out. The customers loved it so much that the owner put it on the menu. "Everybody claimed to be the original," Garagiola said. "The original was down in Oldani's." Most today seem to agree with him.

But wait. Some say it happened at Charlie Gitto's, at 5226 Shaw Avenue on the Hill, when it was Angelo's Restaurant. In this telling, a woman was startled and accidentally dropped ravioli in boiling oil. After it was retrieved, it tasted delicious. The origin claims can continue, but all the creation stories share a common theme: toasted ravioli was an accident. Unless it wasn't. After all, gooey butter cake also supposedly was invented by accident. The truth is, nobody knows, which is just as well. It's enough to say the new creation gradually took hold in the neighborhood and became a St. Louis specialty, but it never caught on nationally. Joseph R. DeGregorio, who gives guided tours of the Hill, said that people on his

TOASTED RAVIOLI

tours who come from farther away than 150 miles generally don't know about toasted ravioli. He brings tour groups to Mama Toscano's Ravioli at 2201 Macklind Avenue. In its handmade method, a filling of pork, beef, spinach, onions, carrots, and tomatoes is poured on dough. Then another layer of dough is placed on top. Next, a specially made roller with square indentations is rolled over the mix, stamping out ravioli either for toasting or boiling. After being cut apart, ravioli for toasting is washed with eggs and milk, dipped in breadcrumbs, and frozen. Later, the raviolis are placed in a skillet and fried briefly on either side, preferably with canola oil. Then they are sprinkled with cheese and served with marinara sauce. Other makers produce their toasted ravioli by machine, which results in ridges and a crustier and harder dough. Some restaurants buy toasted ravioli from Mama Toscano's or other places. Others make their own. However they make it, people still are thankful to whoever dropped the ravioli in the wrong pan.

The South Side Shotgun

Gina Meyer loves her house, and she loves the location on the Hill. Besides, it's down the street from Milo's Tavern at 5201 Wilson Avenue, where she tends bar. But there are disadvantages, beginning with the fact that the house is only fourteen and a half feet wide. Anybody who wants to go from the small living room to the dining room, kitchen, and bathroom has to pass through her bedroom. It makes it hard to entertain, she said. Her two daughters live in converted bedrooms in the basement. Things could be worse, though. The kitchen and dining areas originally were in the basement. "I guess it beats an apartment," Meyer said.

Meyer lives in a shotgun house, so named because it is so narrow that a person could shoot a shotgun in the front of a house and see the shot pass through the back. Generally, they don't have hallways. These houses are plentiful on the Hill. The homes began with Italian immigrants who arrived here between 1890 and 1904, said Joseph R. DeGregorio, a second-generation tour guide on the Hill. They lived in shantytowns and boardinghouses while they saved their money to bring their loved ones to America. With the close of the 1904 World's Fair, the opportunity came for them to move into something better. All of the structures at the fair had to be dismantled. "There was a lot of free lumber to be had from all those dismantled buildings," DeGregorio said. So they began building homes near the Italian missionary church at Wilson and Marconi avenues near the present site of St. Ambrose Church. These homes were in the shotgun style, since it allowed people to build more homes in a given block. Bricks and concrete later were added to many, along with a second floor to some. Kitchens often were put in the basement, and many of the homes still have kitchens there. Many of the front lawns were small with elongated backyards. They had long gardens in the back. Only a couple of shotgun house owners have added a second floor, DeGregorio said, but some of the homes are actually classified as two-story because the basement is street level. Many of the shotgun homes were built on stilts as the basements were filled in later when the owner had the money.

In the spring of 2010, Hill real estate agent Carol Savio was showing a shotgun house in the 5200 block of Botanical Avenue. At twenty feet wide, it was not quite as narrow as Meyer's, but there were distinct signs that this home was built in the shotgun style. The outhouse was in the back. As with many shotgun homes, the kitchen originally was in the basement. The kitchen and bathroom were added on to the back of the house. "People just kept adding on and on," Savio said. Originally, people would have walked into the living room, then the first bedroom, and then the second one. In this house, as in all shotgun houses, people have done work to modernize them.

While shotgun houses are typically associated with the Hill, they are common throughout the South Side. One of them is not far from the Bevo Mill. Ryan Calaway lives in a fifteen-foot-wide frame shotgun house with his two-and-a-half-year-old daughter, Tristin. It looks uncomfortably small on the outside. But on the inside, it is surprisingly spacious. "It's a tiny house, but for the two of us, we're not too crowded," said Calaway. An open kitchen is behind the living room. Calaway and his daughter live in the bedroom behind that. "I don't know that I would stay here forever, but really, it's been ideal for the last five or six years of my life." He paid $59,500 for it at the height of the real estate bubble and got back a $5,000 rebate for rehab work. It may be high in 2010 dollars, but it's still one of the lowest prices around for a house. With Calaway and other buyers of shotgun houses, that's the biggest attraction.

Pretzel Men

A gaunt man with a graying beard and a ponytail looks at northbound motorists who have just exited Interstate 55 and are preparing to turn left onto Loughborough Avenue. Then a woman motions to him. She gives him five dollars. In return, he gives her six pretzel sticks individually bagged so they are not soiled by his hands. "Ain't too much to smile about. It don't look like I'm going to make forty dollars today," Charles Boyd said. On a good night, he can make forty dollars between 4 p.m. and 7 p.m. after deducting his costs. But this wasn't a good night. He's bought the pretzels for twenty-five cents each from Gus' Pretzels store at 1820 Arsenal Street. "I made more money panhandling this corner than I did selling pretzels," Boyd said. One reason is the vendor's license Boyd wore around his neck. It set him back two hundred dollars. He also had to sign up to pay sales tax. Otherwise a cop might see him and haul him in.

Once, people like Boyd sold pretzels everywhere on South Side street corners. Gus Koebbe Jr., who owns Gus' Pretzels, said one reason for the change is laws that make it more difficult for people just to go buy pretzels and start selling them. Those include restrictions on where they can sell and vendors' licenses. "Now, a lot of people don't want to be standing on the street corners," he said. He estimates about a half-dozen people buy from him. But big profits still are possible. Street vendors buy anywhere from fifty to five hundred pretzels and sell them for a dollar each. On Loughborough, Jamieson Avenue, and Hampton Avenue, there are much fewer pretzel sellers than there once were, but those who look will still find them.

Koebbe knows what the pretzel vendor goes through. He easily could have made enough for soda and candy by selling newspapers, but his father— Gus Koebbe Sr.—wouldn't hear of it. After all, Gus Sr. was the second generation in the family business known then and now as Gus' Pretzels. So Gus' father gave him a supply of stick pretzels and sent him out to sell them. Back in 1964, when Koebbe was eight, pretzels wholesaled for two-and-a-half cents and retailed for a nickel. Today, they're a quarter in lots of one hundred or more. He found plenty of takers among people building

an Arsenal Street bridge over the new Interstate 55. At a high school football game, he could sell five hundred pretzels in two-and-a-half hours. Koebbe, who stopped selling when he went into high school, didn't do as well at some street corners. Sometimes it would take him four or five hours to sell a couple of hundred at a slow corner. It was still enough to keep him in pocket money.

The tradition of selling pretzels on the street enabled Koebbe's grandfather, Frank Ramsperger, to make a living after he lost the use of an eye in an accident at his job as a riveter. He started baking pretzels. "Back in those days, you could make stuff at your home and go sell it at the corner," Koebbe said. Eventually, he got a shop. In 1942, Koebbe's grandfather bought the building where the pretzels are made now. Ten years later, Koebbe's father and mother bought the business and gave it the name it has now. Today, under the leadership of Gus Jr., the company makes about forty-eight to fifty thousand pretzels a week. "We go through a couple hundred sacks of flour a week," Koebbe said. Many of the finished products go into stores around the area. Besides regular pretzels, people who come to Gus' Pretzels can buy cinnamon sugar pretzels, garlic pretzels, and salsiccia, bratwurst, hot dog, and deli pretzels. By special order, they can buy pretzel numbers and letters, eighteen-inch pretzels, and twelve-inch pretzels. "We've never had it. This is the first time," Malik Jones said as he brought his family in to the main store. Later, as they ate their pretzels in their van in the store's parking lot, they made a decision. "Good. I like it," Jones said. But it's not quite the same as when you buy it from a vendor on the street.

Gus Koebbe Jr.

Corkball

As with so many stories on the South Side, this one begins at the brewery. Around 1904, employees of Anheuser-Busch decided they needed something to do at lunchtime. So they whittled balls out of the cork bungs that plugged the holes in their beer barrels. They used broom handles for bats and came up with a form of baseball that's still distinctive to St. Louis and the South Side. There's no running, only a pitcher, hitter, and catcher. Fielders are nice additions, but the number of them is optional. The ball looks like a baseball but is only two inches in diameter, or just bigger than a golfball. The bat is thirty-eight inches long and two inches thick, not much larger than the broom handles first used to play the game. The game is still played at places such as Tower Grove Park, Jefferson Barracks, and a field on Walsh Street just east of Ulena Avenue used by the Gateway Corkball Club.

Just before 7 on a Wednesday night in June, members of the Gateway Corkball Club gathered in seats behind two pitchers' mounds in the midst of a neatly kept grass field. Four teams of six played, two at each combination of mounds, batters' boxes, and plates. Marty Kirner, a sales representative who lives in St. Louis Hills, was one of those players. His father—city police officer and Alderman Dan Kirner—long played for the club, so Marty joined in college. "With the club, there's several generations," said Marty, who's been playing for twenty-seven years. "My brother and I play. There's a lot of fathers and grandfathers," said Marty, who has been a club batting champion for more than ten years. Mike Moehlenbrock, a great nephew of Dan Kirner, is among Marty's relatives in the Corkball Club. Mike stopped playing baseball in college and started playing corkball when he turned twenty-one.

Jack Buck, no relation to the broadcaster, is among the old timers on the team. "This league actually started in 1929," said Buck, who has been playing for at least forty years. He pitched until about ten years ago and was club pitching champ in 1993. The names of each year's batting, pitching, and catching champs going back to 1930 are listed on plaques on the wall of the group's clubhouse next to the field. The group started using that field in the 1950s.

Today, the team has about seventy-five active members, although some just drink and play cards in the clubhouse. "It's one of those things I just count on doing Wednesdays," said club vice president John Moeser, whose grandfather used to be a member. "I have to explain it to everybody," Moeser said. When they understand the rules, they're hooked, he said. Among those rules: games are five innings long. A swing and a miss on the first strike is an out, as long as the catcher catches it. A called or swinging strike on the second pitch is an out, as long as the catcher holds it. Any third strike is an out. Five balls over the strike zone is a walk. A foul ball is an out. Whether a hit ball is a single, double, or triple depends on how far it goes. A home run is over a building at the edge of the field. If a batter is hit, it's the same as a walk. "If it hits on the edge of a bone, it's ugly," Buck said. There are two ten-week seasons, and the winners of the first half play the winners of the second half. Then there's an all-star game and a tournament involving teams from all over the area around Labor Day.

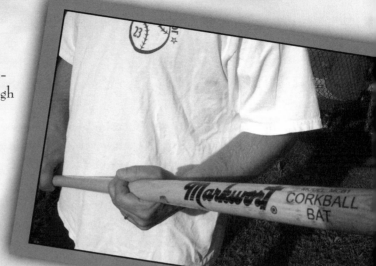

Corkball isn't as big a game as it once was. After World War II, each of about forty taverns in the city organized enclosed "cages" to play the game. Outside of St. Louis, there are indications it was played in places as far apart as Peoria, Illinois, Jacksonville, Florida, and even Egypt. Possibly, it was spread by servicemen in World War II. According to one story, a sailor was amazed no one on his ship had heard of a corkball. So he asked his mother to send him a corkball and corkball bat so he could show his fellow sailors how to play. Today, those bats and balls are made in China—where else?—for Markwort Sporting Goods Co. of St. Louis. The company's corkball logo includes the words "St. Louis's Classic Baseball Game"—to which someone south of Highway 40 would add, "The South Side's Classic Baseball Game."

Gumballs on the Sidewalk

On a tree-lined street in the Bevo Mill neighborhood, a couple live a mostly contented life in a frame house with two cats. Not that there's anything unusual about living on a tree-lined street on the South Side. The Forestry Division of the St. Louis Department of Parks, Recreation and Forestry maintains about eighty thousand trees between sidewalks and curbs. They add beauty to city life, not to mention shade to relieve the hottest August day. But here is where the couple's contented life becomes mostly contented. Two thousand of the city's eighty thousand trees are the dreaded sweetgums, carriers of the cursed sweet gumballs. One of those trees is in front of the couple's house. One is next door. As regular as swallows returning to Capistrano, the dreaded balls start falling in front of the couple's house in the days after Christmas. The fibrous ugly brown balls with lots of spikes on them drop from different trees at different times. But at their house, they first appear as the couple dump the last of the paper from unwrapped gifts in the trash. First one or two, then a dozen. Then mountains of balls ready to turn up the ankles of those foolish enough to step on one. If they're raked in the morning before work, more are on the sidewalk after work. If they're not raked for two, three, or more days, they collect, crying out to the neighbors, "These people don't care."

Almost everybody hates sweetgum trees, but South Siders have a particular reason to despise them. By planting them at the curb, the city guaranteed that the gumballs would stand out horribly when they fell on the sidewalk and street. Amazingly, though, one South Sider—Chip Tynan—doesn't mind them. A horticulturist, he manages the Missouri Botanical Garden's Horticultural Answer Service. Every morning from 9 a.m. to noon, master gardeners answer questions on topics like why weeds keep coming back to their lawn to how to make their daisies better. They may even take questions about what to do about their sweetgum trees. Tynan knows it won't make him popular, but he actually loves the trees. "People think I'm nuts when I say that I like sweetgum trees," he said. "Anybody who sees a sweetgum in its autumn color has to be struck by how beautiful the tree is." The tree is seen in sites from Connecticut to Southern Illinois to Central Florida and Northeastern Mexico. It grows

big, and it grows fast. With it comes the balls—fruits, really—containing individual capsules of seeds that fall out of the balls. In mid- to late April, small greenish flowers form. By the time the gumballs fall from the tree, the seeds are long gone. Actually, birdwatchers should like them. Songbirds like the seeds. So do goldfinches, housefinches, and purple finches.

First cultivated in 1681, the trees are used commercially for pulp, lumber, and veneer. Missouri Botanical Garden founder Henry Shaw included sweetgums in the list of trees to be planted when he developed Tower Grove Park. At one time people included sweetgums on a list of good street trees. Very few kinds of trees can survive well between streets and sidewalks. Tynan hesitates to criticize the city for planting the trees but agrees the balls pose a problem at those spots. Among those problems are how to dispose of them. It can take years for them to break down in a compost pile. "It's one of the few items that I've ever fed into a chipper shredder and had it emerge out the other end almost intact."

Tynan has heard of people sticking them together with wax for a fire starter. They also make great tabletop Christmas trees. Just put them into a pyramid, stick them together with a glue gun, and spray on white paint to give a frosted effect. Placed on the top of a flowerbed, they can keep away cats and rabbits, or so the story goes. Something called the Nut Wizard is supposedly great for picking up acorns, walnuts, and gumballs without bending over. These can be effective, Tynan said, but added, "People are always looking for a reason not to go out and use a rake." A hormonal spray is said to reduce the number of flowers and thereby the number of balls. But it's nasty on metal paint, especially the finish of your neighbor's BMW, Tynan said. He recommends that professionals do the job. Even then, there's no guarantee the product will work. It has to be applied when the tree is at full bloom. This once caused consternation to a forestry service that was asked to spray four or five trees, each of which bloomed at a different time.

One effective way to get rid of the menace is to chop the trees down. A disadvantage to this solution is that it's illegal without a permit. For what it's worth, the maximum penalty for violating any city ordinance is a mere five hundred-dollar fine, court costs, and ninety days in jail. City judges usually don't put people in jail for violating ordinances. Exasperated homeowners might consider it a reasonable expense. However, another disadvantage to this is that a tree chopped down next to a street may land on a neighbor's car. It's possible to avoid most neighbors' cars by performing the chore on street cleaning day, when people are issued tickets for not moving their cars from the street. On the other hand, it's still dangerous. If anybody was stupid enough to do this, the authorities doubtless would get out their law books and find violations that would cost somebody much more than a five hundred-dollar fine, court costs, and ninety days in jail. So don't do this. Or don't say where you got the idea.

In the long run, the best way to deal with the mess from sweetgum trees is not to plant them. That's what the city is doing. Although they're good trees for shade, the city's Forestry Division has given up on planting them between sidewalks and streets, Forestry Commissioner Greg Hayes said. But they're still planted in parks. "We get a lot of complaints," Hayes said. The city's pledge not to plant any more sweetgum trees isn't enough for the couple in Bevo Mill who already have two sweetgum trees in front of their house. To them, the trees are part of the passing of the seasons. The balls start to fall after Christmas. The fall continues through the cold and into the start of spring. Then the leaves come out and the falling stops. The leaves provide the front yard with a deep shade into the fall, when they turn golden. Then they fall and are raked away. The tree is barren as Thanksgiving turkey goes on the table and as guests arrive for the couple's early December Christmas party. They mail Christmas letters and buy gifts for relatives in distant cities. Then the day comes, and they open packages they've received from afar. That night, after watching Clarence once again save Jimmy Stewart from making a big mistake, they rest in a satisfied sleep. The next morning, the man heads outside to pick up his paper. On the sidewalk he spies his first gumball. So ends one passage around the sun. So, on the South Side, begins another.

Acknowledgments

Before anyone else, I must acknowledge the love and encouragement of my wife, Lorraine, both in this project and in our thirty years of marriage. She discovered countless typos and mistakes in her thorough Sunday night proofreading sessions before we e-mailed the week's work to Reedy Press. While I was busy interviewing, researching, or writing, she did an endless amount of chores I should have done, including raking up the gumballs that fell into our yard from the sweetgum trees out front. In addition, I can't forget my editor, Matt Heidenry, for skillfully directing me through this process, the efforts of Josh Stevens to market it, and the willingness of both to allow me to write for them.

My editors at the *Suburban Journals* deserve thanks for allowing me to report about St. Louis's South Side since 2001. They are Jim Rygelski, Buck Collier, Jeff Tobin, Monika Kleban, Carolyn Marty, and Jack Cowan. During that time I learned about many of the things covered in this volume and developed a number of the impressions reflected herin. Inevitably, some of the topics covered herein also were subjects of articles I wrote for the *Suburban Journals*. However, in all but a few instances, the research and reporting for the essays in this book are new. The bibliography contains a list of the essays that originally appeared in other forms in the *Journals*, along with the dates of other articles I wrote that I consulted for reference. Thanks to *Suburban Journals* Mid-Metro Managing Editor Carolyn Marty and *Suburban Journals* Editorial Director Dave Bundy for granting me permission to use that material.

Librarians Adele Heagney, Louise Powderly, and Cynthia Millar did a terrific job of finding research materials for me in my regular visits to the St. Louis Public Library's Central Branch; so did Ron Bolte and the other faithful volunteers at the Carondelet Historical Society. Others who deserve mention include Charles E. Brown, assistant director of the St. Louis Mercantile Library, the staff of the city Board of Public Service, Catherine A. Smentkowski, the many who granted me interviews, and countless others who helped along the way.

Finally, thanks to you, for buying and reading this book. If something you read here adds to your knowledge, makes you think, or brings a smile, I've done my job.

Bibliography

Three essays in this book are revised versions of articles previously published in the *Suburban Journals*, with additional material added. They are the ones on Chic Young, South Side boxing, and Betty Grable. They are used by permission.

Interviews

Mark Abbott, professor of history, Harris-Stowe State University, May 7, 2010.

Michael Allen, architectural historian, January 19, 2010.

Barbara Anderson, retired volunteer director, St. Louis Psychiatric Rehabilitation Center, April 9, 2010.

Brad Arteaga, photographer, May 4, 2010.

Eldon Arteaga, photographer, May 4, 2010.

Josh Boeks, manager, nine St. Louis recreation centers.

Ron Bolte, president, Carondelet Historical Society, March 20, 2010, and other times.

Charles Boyd, pretzel salesman on Idaho Avenue at Loughborough Avenue.

Pat Brannon, owner, Casa Loma ballroom, May 29, 2010.

John "Jack" Buck, Brian McCarthy, Marty Kirner, Matt Klein, Mike Moehlenbrock, John Moeser, members, Gateway Corkball Club, June 9, 2010.

Ryan Calaway, Bevo Mill shotgun homeowner, May 23, 2010.

Bob Corbett, Dogtown resident and historian.

Slim and Zella Mae Cox, gospel singers and Chippewa Street furniture dealers.

Debra Craig, Marquette Recreation Center director; Joseph Dunlap, coach, Marquette Recreation Center boxing program; Danny McGinnist, volunteer, Marquette Recreation Center boxing program; Jarvis Williams, boxer in the program, interviewed about Marquette Recreation Center boxing program.

Anna Crosslin, president and chief executive officer, International Institute, St. Louis, May 5, 2010.

Stephen Conway, 8th Ward alderman.

Billie Ferguson, owner, Ferguson's Pub, March 7, 2010, along with customers John Dennis, "Brian" and waitress Barb Gannon.

Andy Colligan, Missouri Botanical Garden archivist.

Florence Deppe, Betty Reinbold, and Virginia Palazzolo, residents of the Altenheim, 5408 S. Broadway.

Fati Dime, owner, Cisse's Fashion and Hair Braiding Salon, May 6, 2010.

Jennifer Florida, 15th Ward alderwoman, May 2, 2010.

Rita Ford, president, Gravois Park Neighborhood Association, June 5, 2010.

Mark Rice, former volunteer with the Chippewa Street Frog Garden.

Mickey Garagiola, brother of Joe Garagiola, May 1, 2010.

Esley Hamilton, preservation historian, St. Louis County Department of Parks, January 19, 2010.

Mike Howard, Dolores Morfia and Billy Watkins, at Five Star Senior Center, June 11, 2010; and

Don L. O'Toole Jr., all about Bucket Joe.

Greg Hayes, commissioner, Forestry Division, City of St. Louis.

Andrea Hunter, tribal history preservation officer, Osage Nation, June 7, 2010.

Ruth Kamphoefner, Lafayette Square pioneer, April 27, 2010.

John Karel, director, Tower Grove Park, April 6, 2010.

Dorothy Kirner, Former 25th Ward alderwoman.

Gus Koebbe Jr., owner of Gus' Pretzels.

Katherine Kozemczak, volunteer at Chatillon-DeMenil Mansion, May 29, 2010.

Arlene Kruse, owner, Kruse Gardens, Columbia, Ill.; Evan Ely, Tower Grove South; Scott Androff, photographer; Matt Leitch; and Yolanda Thompson, on May 22, 2010 in Soulard Market.

Sadic Kukic, Bosnian restaurant owner, April 24-25, 2010.

Marty and Sue Luepker, owners, Al Smith's Feasting Fox Restaurant, along with customers.

Sue Maehl, former resident of house on top of Sugarloaf Mound, June 7, 2010.

Bruce Marren, nephew of Mickey Garagiola, May 1, 2010.

Mickey McTague, numerous interviews.

Gina Meyer, owner of Hill neighborhood shotgun house, May 5, 2010.

Steve Mizerany, appliance dealer, May 24, 2010.

Vince Mizerany, son of Steve Mizerany, May 24, 2010.

Robert Moll, Tower Grove East Neighborhood resident.

Bob Morris, friend of Steve Mizerany, May 24, 2010.

Monsignor Sal E. Polizzi, Hill neighborhood community leader during battle to erect the Edward Street Overpass over Interstate 44, June 8, 2010.

Lewis Reed, Board of Alderman president, May 6, 2010.

Carol Savio, Hill neighborhood real estate agent, May 6, 2010.

Craig Schmid, 20th Ward alderman.

James F. Shrewsbury, former Board of Aldermen president.

Dan Sinclair, son of Dave Sinclair, April 7, 2010.

Francis G. Slay, mayor of St. Louis, Jan. 26, 2010.

South Siders Mike Carril, Julie McNeal, Norma King, "Glenn" and Van Johnson, asked about definition of "Hoosier."

Carol Surgant, daughter of Ruth Kamphoefner, Lafayette Square pioneer.

Harry Swanger, Compton Heights Neighborhood resident.

Kacie Starr Triplett, 6th Ward alderwoman.

Chip Tynan, manager of the horticulture answer service, Missouri Botanical Garden, May 6, 2010.

Steve Vollenweider, organizer of benefit for American Diabetes Association, May 29, 2010.

Todd Waelterman, St. Louis Street Commissioner, late April 2010.

Brian Wahby, chairman, St. Louis Democratic Committee.

Fred Wessels, 13th Ward alderman.

Canon Michael K. Wiener, rector, St. Francis de Sales Oratory, May 4, 2010.

Phyllis Young, 7th Ward alderwoman.

Walt, Kim and Danny Wiseman; Pete, Pat and David Lecko; Marguerite Still; and Melissa Hegerstroem, all interviewed at Ted Drewes, 6726 Chippewa Street, May 15, 2010.

Joseph Winkler, manager, research collections, St. Louis Public Library, July 24, 2010.

Books

Conley, Timothy G. *Lafayette Square: An Urban Renaissance*. St. Louis: Lafayette Square Press, 1974.

Curzon, Julian, editor and compiler. *The Great Cyclone at St. Louis and East St. Louis, May 27, 1896: Being a Full History of the Most Terrifying and Destructive Tornado in the History of the World*. Carbondale: Southern Illinois University Press, 1997. Originally published by Cyclone Publishing, St. Louis, 1896.

Faherty, William Barnaby. *Henry Shaw, His Life and Legacies*. Columbia: University of Missouri Press, 1987.

Garagiola, Joe. *Baseball Is a Funny Game*. Philadelphia: Lippincott, 1960.

Griesedieck, Alvin. *The Falstaff Story, Second Edition*. St. Louis, 1952.

Herbst, Henry, Don Roussin, and Kevin Kious. *St. Louis Brews: 200 Years of Brewing in St. Louis, 1809–2009*. St. Louis: Reedy Press, 2009.

Hernon, Peter, and Terry Ganey. *Under the Influence: The Unauthorized Story of the Anheuser-Busch Dynasty*, New York, London, Toronto, Sydney, Tokyo, Singapore: Simon & Schuster, 1991.

Houck, Louis. *A History of Missouri From the Earliest Explorations and Settlements Until the Admission of the State Into the Union, Volume II*. Chicago: R. R. Donnelley & Sons Co., 1908.

Hyde, William, and Howard L. Conard, editors. *Encyclopedia of the History of St. Louis: A Compendium of History and Biography for Ready Reference*. New York: The Southern History Company, 1899.

Jackson, Rex T. *James B. Eads: The Civil War Ironclads and His Mississippi*. Bowie, Md.: Heritage Books, 2004.

Koch, A Ryrie. *Carondelet Yesterday and Today*. St. Louis: unpublished, 1933.

Krebs, Roland, in collaboration with Percy J. Orthwein. *Making Friends Is Our Business: 100 Years of Anheuser-Busch*. St. Louis: Anheuser-Busch, 1953.

Lossos, David A. *St. Louis Casa Loma Ballroom,* Charleston S.C.: Arcadia Publishing, 2005.

Kamphoefner, Ruth, *Lafayette Comes Back*. St. Louis: self-published, 2000.

McAdam, David H. *Tower Grove Park of the City of St. Louis*. Prepared by Order of the Board of Commissioners. St. Louis: R.P. Studley & Co., Printers, 1883.

O'Connor, Msgr. P.J. *History of Cheltenham and St. James Parish, Commemorating the Diamond Jubilee of St. James Parish and the 25th Anniversary of the Coming to the Parish of Rev. P.J. O'Connor, Pastor*. St. Louis, 1937.

O'Neil, Tim. *Mobs, Mayhem & Murder: Tales from the St. Louis Police Beat*. St. Louis: St. Louis Post-Dispatch Books, 2008.

Plavchan, Ronald Jan. *A History of Anheuser-Busch, 1852–1933*. North Stratford, NH: Ayer Company Publishers, Inc., 1969, 2000. Originally published by Arno Press, 1976.

Rother, Hubert and Charlotte. *Lost Caves of St. Louis: A History of the City's Forgotten Caves*. St. Louis: Virginia Publishing, 1996.

Taylor, Philip. *A Brief Description of Soulard Market, Past and Present: Acquisition of Lands Pertaining to the Property, and Items Concerning the Soulard and Cerre Families*: St. Louis: unpublished manuscript, 1975.

Twain, Mark. *Life on the Mississippi*. New York: Harper, 1951.

Weaver, Dwight. *Missouri Caves in History and Legend*. Columbia: University of Missouri Press, 2008.

Young, James A., and Cheryl G. Young. *Seeds of Woody Plants in North America, Revised and Enlarged Edition*. Portland, Ore.: Dioscorides Press, 2009

Newspapers and Other Publications

Alton Telegraph, October 17, 2009.

Bugle, December 1, 1979.

McKinley High School *Carnation*, 1915–19.

Missouri Historical Society Bulletin, July/August 1996.

Missouri Republican, October 1, 1864.

Naborhood Link News, May 9, 1979.

Saint James Parish Newsletter, March 30, 1952.

St. Louis Globe-Democrat, Aug. 30, 1870, Jan. 5, 1872, May 28, 1896, June 7, 1902, Aug. 21, 1915, April 24, 1929, April 28, 1929, June 30, 1929, April 5, 1933, April 7, 1933, April 8, 1933, Nov. 26, 1938, May 27, 1943, March 28, 1946, Aug. 25, 1951, April 25, 1953, April 26, 1953, April 29, 1953, April 30, 1953, May 7, 1953, June 14, 1953, June 26, 1953, Dec. 3, 1953, Jan. 27, 1954, Aug. 8, 1956, Oct. 17, 1957, Oct. 19, 1957, Oct. 22, 1957, Oct. 23, 1957, Nov. 6, 1957, Dec. 18, 1957, Dec. 28, 1957, Nov. 20, 1958, Jan. 20, 1959, Feb. 10, 1959, Feb. 11, 1959, Jan. 13, 1960, Jan. 14, 1960, Feb. 14, 1960, April 17, 1960, May 1, 1960, Jan. 8, 1961, Jan. 22, 1961, April 30, 1961, July 24, 1961, Aug. 20, 1961, Nov. 16, 1961, Jan. 15, 1962, June 7, 1962, Jan. 3, 1963, March 22, 1963, July 21-22, 1963, Aug. 24, 1963, Aug. 29, 1963, Sept. 4, 1963, Jan. 28, 1964, April 8, 1964, June 28, 1964, Oct. 1, 1964, Feb. 24, 1965, April 16, 1965, April 19, 1965, Sept. 29, 1965, Nov. 3, 1965, Dec. 13, 1965, Feb. 18, 1966, May 27, 1966, Sept. 15, 1966, Nov. 6, 1966, Feb 4-5, 1967, Feb. 20, 1967, March 27, 1967, April 16, 1967, May 10, 1967, July 13, 1967, May 3, 1968, July 18, 1968, Sept. 11, 1968, Nov. 26, 1968, Nov. 28, 1968, Dec. 12, 1968, May 19, 1969, June 16, 1969, June 21-22, 1969, June 28-29, 1969, July 19, 1969, Sept. 25, 1969, Dec. 7, 1969, Jan. 16, 1970, March 18, 1970, Jan. 17, 1971, Aug. 27, 1971, June 3, 1975, June 9, 1975, June 13, 1975, Oct. 1, 1975, July 1, 1978, Dec. 10, 1979, Feb. 25, 1980, April 5-6, 1980, May 2, 1980, March 29, 1982, March 30, 1982, , Oct. 13, 1982, Oct. 15, 1982, Jan. 18, 1985, June 17, 1985, Aug. 5, 1986.

St. Louis Post-Dispatch, Jan. 20, 1898, May 19, 1913, Aug. 21, 1915, Aug. 22, 1915, May 9, 1929, March 11, 1933, April 5, 1933, April 7, 1933, April 8, 1933, March 13, 1937,

April 7, 1937, March 6, 1938, March 7, 1945, March 10, 1945, April 4, 1945, March 12, 1949, April 6, 1949, Aug. 24, 1951, Jan. 20, 1959, Jan. 28, 1959, Feb. 10, 1959, Feb. 11, 1959, April 23, 1950, Oct. 8, 1957, Jan. 29, 1958, Dec. 24, 1958, Jan. 14, 1960, Oct. 2, 1960, April 5, 1961, April 30, 1961, Jan. 3, 1962, Jan. 13, 1963, March 10, 1963, July 21, 1963, July 22, 1963, Aug. 4, 1963, March 22, 1964, May 16, 1965, July 20, 1965, July 21, 1965, Aug. 1, 1965, April 3, 1966, May 19, 1967, July 9, 1967. April 9, 1968, March 17, 1969, Aug. 16, 1969, Feb. 11, 1970, June 13, 1971, March 21, 1974, June 13, 1975, June 3, 1977, Nov. 2, 1977, July 27, 1979, March 2, 1980, March 14, 1980, Aug. 14, 1980, Sept. 21, 1980, Dec. 23, 1980, March 29, 1982, March 30, 1982, May 26, 1982, March 9, 1983, April 23, 1983, Aug. 17, 1983, Dec. 16, 1983, June 23, 1985, June 24, 1985, June 26, 1985, June 29, 1985, Nov. 5, 1985, Nov. 14, 1985, Nov. 15, 1985, Oct. 9, 1986, May 9, 1988, Jan. 13, 1989, Dec. 22, 1992, Sept. 7, 1993, Jan. 13, 1995, May 5, 1996, Jan. 1, 1997, Feb 28, 1997, May 28, 1998, Sept. 18, 1998, Nov. 8, 1998, Nov. 9, 1998, Nov. 10, 1998, Nov. 11, 1998, Nov. 13, 1998, Nov. 15, 1998, May 18, 1999, Aug. 22, 1999, Dec. 30, 1999, Jan. 5, 2000, March 7, 2001, March 21, 2001, March 3, 2005, June 2, 2005.

St. Louis Republic, May 28, 1896, Aug. 21, 1915.

St. Louis Star, March 13, 1933.

St. Louis Star-Times, June 20, 1950.

St. Louis Times, Aug. 9, 1911, Aug. 14, 1911.

Southwest City Journal, Aug. 29, 1990.

South Side Edition Suburban Journals, June 24, 2009.

South Side Journal, July 28, 1948, Jan. 3, 1952, March 27, 1994, March 15, 1995, April 14, 1996, Feb. 25, 1998, Jan. 9, 2000, Dec, 19, 2001.

Suburban Journals articles by the author: July 20, 2005, Nov. 28, 2007, March 5, 2008, March 12, 2008, Aug. 20, 2008, Sept. 1, 2008, Oct. 1, 2008, Oct. 22, 2008, Nov. 5, 2008, Dec. 17, 2008, Dec. 31, 2008, Jan. 7, 2009, March 4, 2009, March 25, 2009, April 8, 2009, July 1, 2009, July 10, 2009, Sept. 1, 2009, Sept. 23, 2009, Feb. 23, 2010.

Related Material

Allen, Michael. *A Short History of the City Hospital*, 1995 and 2003.

Blick, Boris, and H. Roger Grant. "French Icarians in St. Louis," *Bulletin*, Missouri Historical Society, October 1973.

Colligan, Andrew, archivist, Missouri Botanical Garden, e-mail to author, July 21, 2010.

Dawn of a New Day for Grand and Gravois, booklet commemorating the opening of South Side National Bank, January 2, 1929.

Drawings of reconstruction of Oregon Avenue between Potomac and Miami streets, 1927–28, provided by staff of President's Office, St. Louis Board of Public Service.

Davis, Mark, Union Pacific spokesman, e-mails to author, May 4, 2010, and June 3, 2010.

Engleman, Glennon, Appelant, v. Ruth M. Engleman; Bill McCarvey; Special Agent Atf; Unknown agents, Sgt. John McGrady, St. Louis County Police Department, Appellees, United States Court of Appeals, Eighth Circuit – 663 F.2d 799 Submitted Nov. 4, 1981. Decided

Nov. 10, 1981, court papers.

The Great St. Louis Bank Robbery, starring Steve McQueen and directed by Charles Guggenheim, 1959.

Josse, Lynne. Landmarks Association of St. Louis, Inc., National Register of Historic Places, Multiple Property Documentation Form, St. Louis, Missouri, Public Schools of William B. Ittner, 1902–1910.

Josse, Lynne. Landmarks Association of St. Louis, Inc., National Register of Historic Places, Nomination Form for South Side National Bank, March 23, 2000.

Facts about the Climatron: Missouri Botanical Garden, fact sheet published by the Botanical Garden around the time it opened. Undated.

"A Game Born in St. Louis," *Missouri Historical Society Magazine*, Spring 1999.

A Historical Look at Al Smith's Feasting Fox on back of menu, Al Smith's Feasting Fox Historic Restaurant & Pub Banquet Facilities, undated.

Jefferson, Albert. *The Negro of Carondelet*. St. Louis: undated.

Longwisch, Cynthia H. Landmarks Association of St. Louis, Inc., *The Early Public Schools of William B. Ittner*, St. Louis, 1897–1901, 1990.

McTague, Mickey, letter to Thomas J. Mullen, Aug. 24, 2001.

Murray, Thomas E. *"You $#%?&?$#% hoosier!": Derogatory names and the derogatory name in St. Louis, Missouri.,* cited by Graf in *The Word Hoosier,* 1987.

National Register of Historic Places Inventory – Nomination Form for Chatillon-DeMenil House, December 1975.

Official Map of the City of St. Louis As Established by the City Charter of 1876. Prepared under the direction of James W. Suelmann, Director of Streets, 2001.

O'Sullivan, Katie, spokeswoman, St. Louis Metropolitian Police, e-mail to author, April 29, 2010.

Polizzi, Sal. E., Monsignor. *The Edwards Street Overpass: A Lesson in Political Expediency*. Research Paper Submitted to the Graduate School of Saint Louis University in Partial Fulfillment of the Requirements for the Degree of Master of Arts in Urban Affairs, 1972.

Rehkopf, Susan, e-mail to Theresa K.M. Danieley, forwarded to Jim Merkel, Jan. 27, 2010.

Roussin, Donald L., Jr., e-mail to Matthew Heidenry, July 21, 2010.

Rother, Charlotte and Hubert E. "Historic Caves of St. Louis, Mo." *Missouri Speleology,* Vol. II, No. 3, July 1970.

Schmid, Craig. *Explanation of Vote Regarding Floor Substitute for Board Bill No. 122 According to Rule 47 of the St. Louis Board of Aldermen*, letter inserted into minutes of Dec. 11, 2001, Board of Aldermen meeting, printed in Dec. 26, 2001 issue of the *City Journal*.

St. Louis City Directory on microfilm 1917, 1951, 1952.

St. Louis City Directory on microfilm, Polk, 1969.

St. Louis Ordinance 36527, approved January 31, 1928.

St. Louis City Revised Code Division 1: Traffic Code.

Undated news release from Rawlings Sporting Goods Co. containing reprinted material on corkball history and rules from Rawlings Roundup, Volume 1954, No. 4.

Feld, Wally, general manager, St. Francis de Sales Oratory, e-mail to author explaining problems with the St. Francis de Sales Church Steeple, May 12, 14, 2010.

Websites

American Experience: Secrets of a Master Builder: How James Eads Tamed the Mighty Mississippi http://www.pbs.org/wgbh/amex/eads.

Anheuser-Busch, *Beer is Back* http://www.anheuser-busch.com/press/beerIsBack.html.

Corbett, Bob, page on Icarians, http://www.webster.edu/~corbetre/dogtown/icarian/icarian.html.

Corbett, Bob, page on Dogtown, http://www.webster.edu/~corbetre/dogtown/dogtown.html.

Excerpts from "A Walk Around the Square" by Thomas Keay, http://lafayettesqr.com/neighorhood/Shared%20Documents/History.aspx

Facebook page about Bucket Joe by southcitystl.com website, http://www.facebook.com/topic.php?uid=2207600760&topic=7879.

Gooey Butter Cake: Gooey Butter Cake History – Gooey Butter Cake Recipe, Copyright 2004 by Linda Stradley, http://whatscookingamerica.net/History/Cakes/GooeyButterCake.htm.

Graf, Jeffrey, *The Word Hoosier*, Reference Department Herman B. Wells Library Indiana University – Bloomington http://www.indiana.edu/~librcsd/internet/extra/hoosier.html.

International Institute of St. Louis, www.iistl.org.

National Weather Service page on major St. Louis tornadoes http://www.crh.noaa.gov/lsx/climate/torcli/city.php.

Osage Nation, Video recorded during an all employee meeting on August 18, 2009, at the Wah-Zha-Zhi Cultural Center. Sugarloaf Mound and its relation to the Osage Nation was discussed by tribal history preservation Officer, Dr. Andrea Hunter of the Ozark Nation Historic Preservation Office, http://www.osagetribe.com/executive/welcome_sub_page.aspx?subpage_id=54.

Osage Nation, Sugarloaf Nation Comes Home, news release, July 31, 2009, http://www.osagetribe.com/executive/news_story.aspx?news_id=1522.

River des Peres Watershed Coalition: Introduction – River Timeline, http://www.thegreencenter.org/rdp/introduction/timeline.asp.

1916 River des Peres Plan in St. Louis *Summary of Historic Planning Documents*, http://stlouis.missouri.org/government/duffy/riverfront.htm.

Schmidt, Louis, The Confederate Raid in Dogtown on September 29, 1864,

http://www.websteruniv.edu/~corbetre/dogtown/history/schmidt/schmidt3.html.

Soulard Market, http://stlouis.missouri.org/citygov/soulardmarket.

St. Francis de Sales Oratory, http://www.institute-christ-king.org/stlouis.

St. Louis Business Journal, City Hospital transformed into The Georgian condominiums October 13, 2004 http://stlouis.bizjournals.com/stlouis/stories/2004/10/11/daily48.html.

St. Louis Psychiatric Rehabilitation Center history page, http://dmh.mo.gov/slprc/history.htm.

St. Louis Public Library index of St. Louis street names, http://www.slpl.lib.mo.us/libsrc/streets.htm.

St. Louis Public Library, The Naked Truth page, http://exhibits.slpl.org/germanamerican/data/SiteDetail240012748.asp.

Ted Drewes, http://www.teddrewes.com.

Wayman, Norbury L., History of St. Louis Neighborhoods, on St. Louis City neighborhoods history website, http://stlouis.missouri.org/neighborhoods/history.